CAMBRIDGE LIBRAF

Books of enduring sch

Cambridge

The city of Cambridge received its royal charter in 1201, having already been home to Britons, Romans and Anglo-Saxons for many centuries. Cambridge University was founded soon afterwards and celebrated its octocentenary in 2009. This series explores the history and influence of Cambridge as a centre of science, learning, and discovery, its contributions to national and global politics and culture, and its inevitable controversies and scandals.

Girton College 1869-1932

Barbara Stephen (1872–1945) studied history at Girton College, Cambridge, from 1891 to 1894. This history of the college, first published in 1933, drew on her previous publication *Emily Davies and Girton College* as well as on college reports, letters to and from the founders, and information obtained from staff of the college. The college was established on 16 October 1869 by Emily Davies and Barbara Bodichon, and was the first Cambridge college for women students. Women were not admitted to full degrees at Cambridge until 1948, after Stephen's death, though Oxford had awarded degrees to women since 1920. The author probably never imagined that Girton would admit male undergraduates, as it has from 1979. Stephen's informative short history of the college's first sixty years is an intriguing document for those interested in the history of the University of Cambridge or of women's education.

Cambridge University Press has long been a pioneer in the reissuing of out-of-print titles from its own backlist, producing digital reprints of books that are still sought after by scholars and students but could not be reprinted economically using traditional technology. The Cambridge Library Collection extends this activity to a wider range of books which are still of importance to researchers and professionals, either for the source material they contain, or as landmarks in the history of their academic discipline.

Drawing from the world-renowned collections in the Cambridge University Library, and guided by the advice of experts in each subject area, Cambridge University Press is using state-of-the-art scanning machines in its own Printing House to capture the content of each book selected for inclusion. The files are processed to give a consistently clear, crisp image, and the books finished to the high quality standard for which the Press is recognised around the world. The latest print-on-demand technology ensures that the books will remain available indefinitely, and that orders for single or multiple copies can quickly be supplied.

The Cambridge Library Collection will bring back to life books of enduring scholarly value (including out-of-copyright works originally issued by other publishers) across a wide range of disciplines in the humanities and social sciences and in science and technology.

Girton College
1869-1932

BARBARA STEPHEN

CAMBRIDGE
UNIVERSITY PRESS

CAMBRIDGE UNIVERSITY PRESS

Cambridge, New York, Melbourne, Madrid, Cape Town, Singapore,
São Paolo, Delhi, Dubai, Tokyo

Published in the United States of America by Cambridge University Press, New York

www.cambridge.org
Information on this title: www.cambridge.org/9781108015318

© in this compilation Cambridge University Press 2010

This edition first published 1933
This digitally printed version 2010

ISBN 978-1-108-01531-8 Paperback

GIRTON COLLEGE
1869–1932

LONDON
Cambridge University Press
FETTER LANE

NEW YORK · TORONTO
BOMBAY · CALCUTTA · MADRAS
Macmillan

TOKYO
Maruzen Company Ltd

THE FIRST BUILDINGS, 1874

GIRTON COLLEGE
1869-1932

by

BARBARA STEPHEN

CAMBRIDGE
AT THE UNIVERSITY PRESS
1933

To

The Students of Girton College

PAST, PRESENT, AND

TO COME

CONTENTS

PREFACE

THIS SHORT HISTORY of Girton College is based as regards earlier years (Chapters I–V and part of Chapter VI) on my book, *Emily Davies and Girton College*, published in 1927 by Messrs Constable. For the later chapters I have drawn on the Annual Reports of the College; the *Girton Review*; letters from Miss Davies and Miss Metcalfe to Madame Bodichon, lent by her nephew, Mr Valentine Leigh Smith; letters to Madame Bodichon from Miss Marks (Mrs Ayrton), lent by her daughter, Mrs Ayrton Gould; and information supplied by the Librarian of Girton, Miss McMorran, and by the Secretary, Miss Clover, and her assistant, Miss Peace: to all of whom I offer my thanks. I must also thank the Mistress of Girton, Miss Jex-Blake, Miss Major, and Miss Bacon, for criticisms and suggestions.

BARBARA STEPHEN

December 1932

PLAN OF THE COLLEGE

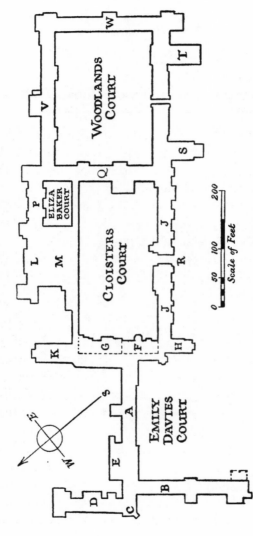

A. Old wing.
B. Hospital wing.
C. Taylor knob.
D. Orchard wing.
E. Chemical laboratory.

F. Old dining hall.
G. Old kitchens.
H. Stanley Library.
J.J. Tower wing.
K. Swimming bath.

L. Kitchens.
M. Dining hall.
P. Fellows' dining room and parlour.
Q. Chapel wing.

R. Main entrance.
S. Chapel.
T. Library.
V. Woodlands wing.
W. New wing.

CHAPTER I

INTRODUCTION

Different origins of men's and women's colleges. Women in the
nineteenth century. The women's movement and its founders. The
founders of Girton. First steps towards higher education.

THE WOMEN'S COLLEGES at the older Universities are now so well established as to be taken for granted as a necessary part of the national system of education. Their character and aims are so far similar to those of the men's Colleges as to obscure at first sight the fact that they are totally different in origin and history. These differences of course leap to the eye so far as the buildings are concerned; and they must be explained if we are to understand their present character and position.

When Girton College was founded in 1869, the University of Cambridge was still in the midst of that remarkable process of change which was to transform its character in the course of the nineteenth century. With five hundred years of life behind it, it was entering upon a fresh chapter and renewing its vitality, after the stagnant period of the eighteenth century, with its sinecures and its narrow exclusiveness.

The origins of the University can be traced back to the thirteenth century; many of the Colleges date from the Middle Ages, and most of them had come into existence before the Reformation. Their main object in the first instance was to encourage learning, for the advancement of knowledge, and with a view to preparing men for the learned professions, especially for teaching and for the priesthood. At a time when the wealthier classes were hardly expected to be literate, it was natural that the students should be drawn from among the poorer classes, and we find that King's College, to take but one instance, was founded by Henry VI for poor scholars who intended to take Holy Orders. Among the wealthier classes there were men and women of enlightened public spirit, kings and queens and princes of the Church, by whose initiative the Colleges were founded. From such beginnings the Universities of Oxford and Cambridge were gradually developed through the Renaissance, the Reformation, the Civil Wars, and all the vicissitudes of English history. Till well on in the nineteenth century they retained their close connection with the Church. Dissenters were not admitted to degrees or to Fellowships. The abolition of religious tests was only carried, after a long agitation, in 1871; and the medieval prohibition of the marriage of Fellows was not withdrawn at Cambridge till 1882. These events formed part of the process by which profound changes were brought about in the Universities, partly by a movement from within, partly by Royal Commissions and Acts of Parliament. By the end of the nineteenth century they were freed from ecclesiastical control, and had become the keystone of the national system of education which had meanwhile been built up. They were regarded not only as leading to the learned professions, but as a normal means, open to young men of all classes and creeds, of preparation for life in general. And with the modern developments of both natural sciences and humane learning, their function of advancing knowledge became of immense value and importance to a far wider circle of students than ever before.

It was during the last thirty years of the nineteenth century, when the Universities were in the thick of this movement, that the women's Colleges were founded. Public opinion was at this time overwhelmingly against the admission of women, not only to the priesthood, but to any of the learned professions. The sole exception—the teaching profession —could not be called learned where women were concerned, as women teachers were in general quite unqualified for their work. The condition and status of women have undergone a revolution during the last sixty years—a revolution in which the women's Colleges have been a powerful though silent force; and the problems which confronted the founders of these Colleges cannot be understood without some reference to the condition of women previous to their foundation.

Such progress as was made in national development during the earlier part of the nineteenth century hardly touched women. The enlargement of the franchise affected them not at all; the same may be said of the growth of education. The freedom of movement made possible to men by improved means of communication and the more complete establishment of law and order was denied to women by custom and tradition; and the developments in trade and industry altered their position only for the worse.[1] While men were advancing, women were standing still—not only standing still, but losing ground. And so it came about that the principal founders of Girton, Emily Davies and Barbara Leigh Smith (Madame Bodichon), were born into a world in which women were generally regarded as hopelessly and by nature inferior to men in intellectual powers as well as in physical strength. There were, of course, notable exceptions; but by the average Englishman the inferiority of "the weaker sex" was taken for granted.

Barbara Leigh Smith, the elder of these two founders, came from a family with strongly progressive traditions, both political and religious. Florence Nightingale was her cousin and contemporary, George Eliot one of her most intimate friends. An unconventional father allowed her to have a good education and a very unusual degree of personal independence, and her gifts of character enabled her to make the fullest use of these advantages. Independent, original, enthusiastic, and generous to a fault, she was full of schemes to reform the world, but she was no unpractical visionary; and her strong cheerful common sense, her wide interests, and her many friends, all helped her to attract support to the unpopular cause of women's education and women's rights. Through her initiative a group was formed of men and women, middle-class Victorians, who were thoughtful enough

[1] This was true of the middle classes, no less than of the wage-earners. See *Emily Davies and Girton College*, Chapter 1.

to see that one of the great needs of their time was the removal of the restrictions which forbade women to receive any education worthy of the name, or to take any active part in the life of their country, not only in politics but even in philanthropy. This group were the pioneers of the modern women's movement.

The movement for the education of women sprang directly from the movement for emancipation generally. In 1856 Miss Leigh Smith, with her friend Miss Parkes (afterwards Madame Belloc), started the first agitation for the reform of the Married Women's Property laws; and in 1858 they established the *Englishwoman's Journal*, the first organ of the women's movement, which led immediately to the foundation of the Society for the Employment of Women. The *Journal* and the Society formed a nucleus from which the many activities of the women's movement grew with extraordinary vigour. It was at once recognized that education was a necessary preliminary to work; women were not employed even in drapers' shops, because they had so little knowledge of arithmetic; and the state of mind of milliners' assistants may be guessed from the notice seen by Charles Dickens in a milliner's window: "Wonted, a feamail Prentis with a Premum".[1] A book-keeping class was started, which grew into a day school; and other developments quickly followed, with profound and far-reaching results. It was at this juncture that a friendship was formed between Miss Emily Davies and

[1] *Letters of Charles Dickens to the Baroness Burdett-Coutts* (John Murray, 1931).

Madame Bodichon, as Miss Leigh Smith had become in 1857, through her marriage to Dr Bodichon of Algiers. Miss Davies was quickly drawn by her new friend into the feminist movement, which all her natural sympathies went forth to meet.

Emily Davies, who was to be the leader of the group which founded Girton, was a woman of remarkable character. She had an inward fire and vision hidden under a carefully conventional exterior. "Her dainty little figure and smiling face", wrote Mrs Townshend, one of the first Girton students, "were most misleading. They concealed untiring energy, a will of iron, and a very clear and definite set of opinions....She was a person of single aim who looked neither to the right hand nor to the left." In all that concerned women, she was a revolutionary; in all else a conservative. And herein lay a great part of her strength, for she was never led to affront the conventions of her time by mere pleasure in affronting conventions. At the same time, she was so fearless and enterprising and far-sighted as to lead the adventure of founding a College for women in connection with one of the older Universities, an adventure which to most of her contemporaries must have seemed, if they were sympathetic, a forlorn hope; if otherwise, a wild-goose chase, or worse. She had the greatness of mind which gave her the vision, the ideal to aim at; she also had the smallness of mind which enabled her to work untiringly at details, in fact to revel in them. Many of her contemporaries saw her as a narrow-minded woman absorbed in these details, and devoted to the unpopular and apparently hopeless task of securing for women admission to the education intended for men. But she was able to gather round her a body of enthusiastic helpers, and eventually to achieve success.

Miss Davies was born a feminist, but her girlhood was passed in surroundings which gave little encouragement to her aspirations. She was the daughter of the Rev. John Davies, Rector of Gateshead from 1839 till 1861. She received the usual education of daughters in those days; that is to say, she was taught almost entirely at home, by her mother and elder sister, with the important addition of "Themes" written once a week for her father, which developed her remarkable power of expressing herself clearly and with force. Through Madame Bodichon, whose acquaintance she made in 1858, she came to know the newly formed band of workers for the women's movement. While living at Gateshead, she could do little to further the cause; but she urged and inspired her friend Miss Elizabeth Garrett (afterwards Mrs Garrett Anderson)[1] to make the attempt to enter the medical profession. With the advice and help of Miss Davies, who came to live in London on her father's death in 1861, Miss Garrett applied in the following year for leave to matriculate at London University. This was refused, and Miss Garrett proceeded on other lines; but Miss Davies determined that University education must be opened to women, and devoted herself thenceforward to working for this object.

[1] See Biographical Index.

A suggestion made at this point by Mr Shaen,[1] of London University, proved fruitful in results, namely, that if something could be got from the older Universities, London might be more likely to prove amenable. The Senior and Junior Local Examinations, established for boys' schools some years previously by the Universities of Oxford and Cambridge, seemed likely to meet the case, as nothing was involved in the way of residence. In October, 1862, a Committee was formed to work for the admission of girls to these examinations. Miss Davies was Secretary, and the other members included Madame Bodichon, Mr Tomkinson, Lady Goldsmid, Mr Heywood, and Mrs Manning, all of whom afterwards took part in the foundation of Girton. Mr Tomkinson was a specially useful ally. Shrewd and humorous, and a very able business man, he was Managing Director of the Sun Insurance Office, and a person of great importance in the insurance world generally. As Bursar of Marlborough he had saved the school from financial disaster and laid the foundations of its prosperity. He had had a very distinguished career at Cambridge; he rowed in the Cambridge eight in 1852, played in the University eleven, and was a Wrangler in 1853. Most fortunately he was in 1862 Secretary for the London centre of the Cambridge Local Examinations for boys. With all these qualifications, he was of course invaluable to the Committee in the delicate task of approaching the Cambridge Local Examinations Syndicate. They would hardly

[1] See Biographical Index.

be likely to listen to a Committee consisting chiefly
of ladies, and bringing forward such very novel proposals, but to Mr Tomkinson they did listen. Leave
was obtained for an experimental examination to be
held for girls; after much anxiety and agitation,
ninety-one candidates were induced to enter, all
difficulties were overcome, and the examination passed
off without a hitch of any kind, Mr Tomkinson afterwards reporting that "there is no ground whatever
for the notion that girls are unfit to take part in these
examinations". The results threw a flood of light on
the poor quality of the teaching in girls' schools, and
the need for the examinations became very apparent.
A memorial was now organized to the University of
Cambridge, and again, after much hard work and
anxiety, success was attained. On March 8th, 1865,
the Senate passed, by a majority of four, a Grace
admitting girls to the Local Examinations. This made
the first contact between women's education and the
Universities.

Meanwhile the way was opening for a step of even
greater importance. In 1864 the Government appointed the celebrated Schools Enquiry Commission
to conduct an exhaustive enquiry into "the whole
subject of middle-class education". Miss Davies
perceived that this offered a golden opportunity, but
she quickly found, to her indignation and disappointment, that "the whole subject of middle-class education" was not going to include the education of
girls. She at once organized an attack in the shape
of a memorial to the Commissioners, which was

successful in its object. Girls were to be included; and women would for the first time in history be called as witnesses before a Royal Commission. Evidence was given by Miss Davies and some others, including the great pioneer headmistresses, Miss Buss, of the North London Collegiate School for Girls, and Miss Beale, of Cheltenham Ladies' College. The Secretary to the Commission, Mr Roby, and an Assistant Commissioner, Mr James Bryce (afterwards Lord Bryce), became great allies of Miss Davies, and later took part in the foundation of Girton. The Commission's Report on girls' education was most fruitful and far-reaching in its results, supplying a powerful stimulus to the movement which brought about the great reformation in girls' schools, without which the work of the women's Colleges could not have been accomplished.

The Schools Enquiry Commission brought Miss Davies into contact with a number of schoolmistresses, who, she found, had been working in isolation, and were anxious for opportunities of co-operation and exchange of ideas with other women teachers. The London Schoolmistresses' Association was organized to meet their needs; among its first members were Miss Buss, Miss Chessar, Miss Manning and Miss Metcalfe—all to be later connected with Girton. The stimulus and encouragement given by this Association was something quite new to women teachers. Miss Davies soon found that what they desired above all things was "something to work up to". An external aim, a goal to achieve, were needed if girls' schools were to be saved from chaos. The Local Examinations were helpful, but something more advanced was wanted—some kind of higher education for which girls could be prepared, and to which they could pass on, after leaving school. Hitherto there had been nothing for them to do but to remain as "daughters at home"—a state which at its best was usually aimless, and at its worst led to idleness and misery. The ablest schoolmistresses of the day felt these difficulties keenly; they sympathized with their girls, but they were handicapped in all directions. Public opinion was against them; and they had the greatest difficulty in obtaining competent teachers. A real demand for higher education was thus arising among thoughtful women concerned with girls' schools, a demand which could not be met by any institution then in existence.

The subject was discussed at a meeting of schoolmistresses held at Manchester on October 6th, 1866, and it was this discussion which, as Miss Davies afterwards wrote, "drove" her to the conclusion that the need could only be met by the foundation of a new College for women. It was a tremendous undertaking; but she flung herself into it with indomitable zeal, and devoted the rest of her long life to its accomplishment.

CHAPTER II

PRELIMINARY WORK FOR THE COLLEGE

First outlines of the scheme. Formation of Committee. Rival principles. The College organized and established at Hitchin.

IT is difficult nowadays to realize the immense obstacles which confronted the would-be founders of a College for women in 1866. To collect money and to organize a College is a difficult task at any time; in those days it was made almost impossible for women by the solid antagonism of public opinion. The alliance between Miss Davies and Madame Bodichon proved remarkably suitable for the attack on this powerful fortress; their qualities were just such as to supplement each other. Miss Davies, as we have seen, had had little in the way of educational opportunities. She was neither a scholar nor a student, and her limitations in this respect made themselves felt after the College had come into being. But she had a genius for organization, and her very advanced views about women being combined with a staunch and even narrow conservatism in other matters formed a combination excellently well suited to the task she had in hand, in her dealings with those whom she was wont to call "the enemy", as well as with those who were merely indifferent or timid. It seemed as though no harm could come, even of such novel ideas, when they were propounded with such skill and propriety by one so orthodox. Madame Bodichon, on the other hand, could never be mistaken for anything but a revolutionary. But she seemed like a being of another order. An artist, and a lover of beauty in all forms, and herself a beautiful woman, she won people to her side by the wideness of her sympathies; kind and firm as she was in the various difficulties which inevitably arose, her genial influence was invaluable, especially in relation to the early generations of students. Unfortunately a serious illness in 1877 cut short her work for the College; but until that date, in spite of her annual visits to Algeria, she was an active and enterprising organizer, and a most helpful influence.

Madame Bodichon naturally entered into the scheme for a women's College with enthusiasm. "I am full of the College", Miss Davies wrote to her in Algeria, "and must discourse about it....Now that the scheme is about to be brought down from the clouds, it seems necessary to make some sort of a statement about it. I have drawn up a Programme of which I enclose a proof....We are told that we ought to ask for £30,000 at least....It is not a large sum...considering how easy it is to raise immense sums for boys' schools. But considering how few people really wish women to be educated, it is a good deal. Everything will depend, I believe, on how we start. If we begin with small subscriptions a low scale will be fixed, and everybody will give in proportion. I mean to give £100, and I believe Lizzie Garrett will do something the same....What we want is a

few promises of large sums, to lead other people on."
Madame Bodichon promised £1000—a sum which
nowadays would seem absurdly small as the nucleus
of a fund for the establishment of a College. But the
idea of spending money on women's education was
so novel that £1000 seemed a very large sum to risk.
It did not, in fact, attract any more thousands; but it
proclaimed the giver's faith in the scheme, and made
a nucleus for the smaller subscriptions by means of
which the College struggled into life.

The "Programme" composed by Miss Davies set
forth the need for higher education and the proposal
to establish a College for advanced students. "Application (she wrote) will be made to the University of
Cambridge to hold Examinations at the College in
the subjects prescribed for the Ordinary (or Poll)
Degree... in the final examinations for which a choice
is offered between Theology, Moral Science...
Natural Science... and other subjects.... There will
also be periodical Examinations in all the subjects
taught in the College, including, in addition
to those above referred to, Modern Languages,
Music, Drawing, and other subjects which usually
form part of the education of an English lady.....
Students will be admitted at the age of sixteen and
upwards."

This preliminary sketch of the College shows how
difficult even Miss Davies found it to get away
from the current ideas as to "the education of an
English lady". It might almost be a description of a
"finishing school" but for the mention of theology and

science.[1] It was an attempt to conciliate public opinion by the bait of "the usual education of an English lady", while offering University examinations to serious students. This was, of course, inconsistent with her true aims; and it was impossible to put into practice, for this reason, that the ladylike subjects, modern languages, music, and history, were not taught in the University at that date. Mathematics and classics held the predominant place, with moral sciences and natural sciences only recently introduced and slowly making their way. Ill-prepared as women students would be, it was too much to ask that they should add to their difficulties by taking extra subjects outside the University curriculum. As for the Tripos examinations, they were assumed—mistakenly as it afterwards proved—to be out of reach so long as girls' schools remained at the low level revealed by the Schools Enquiry Commission.

The scheme, as it stood, plainly would not do; and the Poll examinations themselves were attacked by some of Miss Davies's most important advisers— supporters of University reform who were also interested in the scheme for a women's College. Mr Seeley, Mr Bryce, and Mr Henry Sidgwick, if they could have had their way, would have reformed the Poll examinations, which they heartily despised, root and branch; in the meantime, they felt sure it would be a mistake to tie the new College down to a

[1] Natural sciences were considered to be masculine subjects, though botany and conchology were thought sufficiently elegant for ladies to be allowed to dabble in them.

system which was bad for men, who were at least supposed to be prepared for it, and would be worse for women, who lacked the public school grounding in classics and mathematics. "It would be much better", wrote Mr Bryce, "for a new institution not only to set up a higher standard than the contemptibly low one of Oxford and Cambridge, but to let the examinations be in subjects and on text-books better chosen and of more educational value."

Miss Davies resolutely refused to act on this advice. She saw that it was not practicable to create a new system, for women, of a sufficiently high standard to be of any value. In any case such a standard could not be attained while the education of girls was (as Mr Bryce had shown) at such a very low ebb; and no improvement was practicable in girls' schools without a supply of competent women teachers, who could not be produced without higher education. The higher education must come first, and the practical course was to obtain it from the system already in existence for men, which, though assumed, had never been proved to be unsuitable for women. Moreover, there was no agreement, either among experts or among the public, as to what a special system of education for women should be. The most contradictory theories were constantly produced on the subject. The Poll examinations, bad as they were, were at any rate a known quantity; and if reform were needed, they would be sure to get it—there were high educational authorities who would see to that. Miss Davies therefore was resolved that women students should submit to the same tests, in order that they might share the same opportunities, as men. She kept this constantly in view, and (as will be seen) it needed all her vigilance to prevent her fellow-workers from straying into other paths.

The next step was to organize an Executive Committee for the College. Madame Bodichon, though she was throughout working in close co-operation with Miss Davies, was not one of the first members to join the Committee. She had been prominently connected with the women's suffrage agitation, culminating in the historic election of John Stuart Mill for Westminster in 1865, and in the petition of 1866; and the unpopularity of women's suffrage was such that Miss Davies, with her usual caution, thought it safer that Madame Bodichon's name should not be attached to the College. Her influence proved, however, so valuable as to outweigh this consideration, and she joined the Committee formally in February, 1869. Lady Stanley of Alderley was one of the first invited to join. She was the wife of the second Lord Stanley of Alderley, who had served in the Whig Governments of Lord Melbourne and Lord Palmerston; she had played an important part in politics in the indirect manner open to women of her rank in society (the only political opening for women of that time); and after her husband's death in 1869 she became an active and prominent supporter of women's education. At the moment she declined the invitation to serve on the Executive Committee on the ground that "it is not liked to see my name before the public", but she joined it in 1872. The members who were at once secured were the following:

LADY AUGUSTA STANLEY, a former member of Queen Victoria's household, wife of Dr Stanley, Dean of Westminster.

LADY GOLDSMID, wife of Sir Francis Goldsmid (the first Jew to become a barrister and a member of the House of Commons)—a cultivated and enlightened woman, already a member of the Committee for gaining admission for women to University examinations.

THE DEAN OF CANTERBURY—DR ALFORD—a distinguished Cambridge man, well known as editor of the Greek Testament.

MRS RUSSELL GURNEY (wife of the Recorder of London), who had been helpful to Miss Davies and Miss Garrett in the matter of medical education.

MRS MANNING, the first Mistress of the College.

MISS FANNY METCALFE, one of the few distinguished headmistresses of that day.

MR G. W. HASTINGS, Secretary of the Social Science Association, which had been a powerful aid to the women's movement.

MR JAMES HEYWOOD, M.P., F.R.S., a Unitarian man of business, a supporter of University reform and of women's suffrage.

MR H. J. ROBY, of St John's College, Cambridge, Secretary of the Schools Enquiry Commission of 1864.

MR SEELEY (afterwards Sir John Seeley), Professor of Modern History at Cambridge 1869–95, an ardent University reformer.

MR SEDLEY TAYLOR, of Trinity College, a musician and economist.

This Committee included only two resident members of the University—Mr Sedley Taylor and Mr Seeley. A Cambridge Committee was formed to act in concert with it, consisting of Professor Lightfoot (afterwards Bishop of Durham), three scientific Professors (J. C. Adams, G. M. Humphry, and G. D. Liveing), and eight other members of the University, including Mr (afterwards Professor) Henry Sidgwick, and Mr Sedley Taylor. The last named therefore provided a link between the Executive Committee and the Cambridge Committee.

It was, however, the Executive Committee which carried out all the preliminary work of organization. Its first meeting was held in London on December 5th, 1867. Only Mrs Manning, Mr Sedley Taylor, Mr Tomkinson, and Miss Davies were present. General principles were laid down. The College was to be "if possible, connected with the University of Cambridge", and efforts were to be made to secure the admission of its students to the examinations for degrees of that University. Religious services and instruction were to be in accordance with the principles of the Church of England; and the resident authorities were to be women. To modern ears this last clause sounds superfluous; but in those days it was extremely difficult to find any women suitable to fill such posts, especially as women with academic qualifications did not exist. The religious clause gave some trouble at this stage. "I need not tell you", wrote Mr Bryce to Miss Davies, "that I would far rather there was no mention of one denomination any more than another, but of course you have to look to the practical aspect of the plan, and the feelings of the English upper class. All we care about is that the thing should not seem to be on the face of it—a denominational institution, which is just what Oxford and Cambridge are ceasing to be."[1] Miss Davies, however, held fast to the connection with the Church of England. There was never any difficulty in practice, when once the College was established. Prayers were (and still are) said every morning, and a service conducted on Sundays, but no one was obliged to attend, and students of all denominations were admitted to the College without question.

A letter from Mrs Manning is preserved in the College Library, in which she alludes to this meeting, and announces that she will give £100 to the College funds. A General Committee was gradually got together, which included three bishops, two deans, and other prominent people—enough to give the undertaking an air of solidity and dignity. Of course there were a number of refusals. Most people were disposed to agree with that pillar of orthodoxy, Miss Charlotte Yonge, who wrote to Miss Davies that girls if brought together in large numbers "always hurt one another in manner and tone if in nothing else". Home education, she thought, was "far more valuable both intellectually and morally than any external education.... Superior women will teach themselves, and inferior women will never learn more than enough

[1] The abolition of religious tests at Cambridge was carried four years later, in 1871.

for home life".[1] Though she would have denied it with horror, Miss Yonge's words imply that inferior women will do quite well enough for home life. George Eliot, on the other hand, at Madame Bodichon's instance became a warm supporter of the scheme, subscribed to the funds, and did what she could to help in the campaign which was being carried on by Miss Davies and Madame Bodichon. They were indefatigable agitators, writing and talking about the College incessantly, sending out circulars, and organizing meetings wherever and whenever they could find an opening. These culminated in a meeting in London in March, 1868, attended by about two hundred people, and presided over by the Dean of Canterbury. Speeches were made by Mr Roby, Mr Seeley, Mr Llewelyn Davies, Mr Hastings, Professor Lightfoot, and Mr Tomkinson. No ladies ventured to speak. The small circle who were interested were very zealous, but by the middle of July only about £2000 had been promised, and the £30,000 at which they were aiming remained hopelessly out of sight.

Meanwhile, another group of workers were promoting the education of women on somewhat different lines. Professor Henry Sidgwick, Miss A. J. Clough (sister to the poet Arthur Clough), and others, in 1868 got up a memorial to the Cambridge Senate asking that special examinations might be instituted for women over the age of eighteen. Since the Poll examinations were considered too low, and the Triposes too high in standard for women, the es-

[1] This letter is preserved in the College Library.

tablishment of a special women's examination seemed
to Professor Sidgwick the best way of meeting the
difficulty. Here was Mr Bryce's policy, which Miss
Davies had defeated in her own Committee, coming
to life independently. "It makes me very unhappy",
she wrote to a friend, "to see the Ladies' Lectures,
Ladies' Educational Associations, etc., spreading. It
is an evil principle becoming organized, and gaining
the strength which comes from organization." "We
have not yet come to it in religion," she wrote to
Mr Tomkinson, "but with Ladies' Committees,
Ladies' Associations, Lectures to Ladies, and the rest,
one does not quite see why we should not soon have
also Ladies' Churches and Chapels, in which the
duties of women as such should be specially inculcated. We have the principle already, in the double
moral code, which most people believe in."

Professor Sidgwick was not concerned with the
question of double standards. He wished simply to
give women the best possible education, and then see
what would come of it. If emancipation followed, if
admission to the University followed, well and good,
but the first thing was to try the experiment of education, and to try it in the best possible way. He
carried his point, and the Examinations for Women
were established in 1869.

This was a great blow to Miss Davies; and as the
Executive Committee continued its labour of working
out the College scheme in detail, she found the "evil
principle" raising its head again. Mr Roby, Mr
Tomkinson, and Mr Sedley Taylor drafted a con-

stitution which connected the College vaguely with the three existing Universities (Oxford, Cambridge, and London), while aiming ultimately at the establishment of a separate University for women. Telling Mr Tomkinson that he had gone "terribly astray", she made them draft a new Constitution, setting forth definitely that the aim of the College was "to obtain ...admission to the Examinations for degrees of the University of Cambridge, and generally, to place the College in connexion with that University". Yet again she had to fight for her principles: Mr Seeley, who had been asked to draft a curriculum, reported in favour of a special scheme of studies, far better in his opinion than those of the University. In defiance of his advice, Miss Davies insisted that the students should work for the Cambridge examinations, including those for the despised Poll Degree. She only compromised so far as to allow that the new College should offer "College Certificates" for proficiency in special subjects not included in the Cambridge course. This, however, remained a dead letter; the students were not attracted by the offer, and Miss Davies threw all her influence on the side of the Cambridge examinations.

The College scheme was now so far advanced on paper that it was becoming urgently necessary to secure the students and the building which would translate theory into fact. Madame Bodichon wanted the College to be in Cambridge, but more cautious and conventional views prevailed, and it was decided to rent Benslow House, a substantial villa of moderate size on the outskirts of the town of Hitchin. There was great difficulty in finding anyone suitable for the post of Mistress. Miss Davies fortunately succeeded in persuading her old friend Mrs Manning to undertake the task. They had worked together on various Committees, and Mrs Manning knew something of Queen's College for women, and of the Local Examinations. She was a cultivated woman, and something of a scholar, and her dignity, social tact, and sympathetic character would be of great use in dealing with such an unknown quantity as the students. She was elderly and not very strong, and therefore undertook the post for one term only, her step-daughter, Miss Adelaide Manning, coming with her as a temporary student.

The first student to enter herself for the College was Miss Emily Gibson (now Mrs Townshend), a girl just under eighteen, who had been educated at a good school and was longing for further study. Then came a slightly older recruit, Miss Anna Lloyd, a Quaker—"original and amusing," as Miss Davies wrote, "with the hint of seriousness without which amusingness is rather disagreeable". All students were required to pass an Entrance Examination, a point in which Girton was in advance of many of the colleges in the University. Discouraging as this was to the ill-prepared young women of that day, the rule was most strictly adhered to. Eighteen candidates presented themselves for the first Entrance Examination held in London in July, 1869. After it was over, Miss Davies had a little party for the purpose of introducing the students to the Committee, and here we get a characteristic glimpse of Madame Bodichon. "It was then that I first saw Madame Bodichon," wrote Miss Gibson many years afterwards, "and the little talk I had with her made an outstanding event in my life. Her frank, direct manner went straight to my heart. I felt that the College meant a great deal to her, and that it was a great privilege to have a chance of helping to make it a success. I seem to remember that her face was framed in a cottage bonnet that made a halo for her blue eyes and golden hair. She told me that she had been talking to Miss Townshend and felt sure she would be a leading spirit among the students, a sound prophecy, for her interests were wide and her mind original." This showed much penetration on Madame Bodichon's part, for Miss Townshend was not striking either in appearance or manner. She did prove a leading spirit; but her early death cut short a life of promise.

Thirteen of the candidates passed, and two scholarships which had been subscribed for the three years' course were awarded to Miss Townshend and Miss Woodhead. In October three more candidates were examined, including Miss Lumsden (now Dame Louisa Lumsden). A nucleus of students was thus secured; Benslow House was prepared for occupation by a small Committee consisting of Miss Davies, Mrs Russell Gurney, Miss Garrett, and Mrs Austin (an old friend of Miss Davies, of the Gateshead days); and all was now ready for the great experiment to begin on October 16th, 1869.

CHAPTER III

THE COLLEGE IN ITS PIONEER DAYS

The first students. Life at the College, Hitchin. Difficulties as to work. A question of discipline.

T H E first five students were Miss Gibson, Miss Lloyd, Miss Lumsden, Miss Woodhead, and Miss Townshend; besides Miss Manning, who was to be there for only one term, and did not intend to take any examination. Miss Gibson has described her reception by Miss Davies, on her first arrival at Hitchin. Before she had time to knock or ring, "the door was opened, and on the threshold there stood the keen little lady to whose courage and energy the whole scheme of a College for women was due, and who was now quivering with excitement, thinly veiled under a business-like manner, in this moment when her cherished hopes were actually beginning to materialize". Four days later, Miss Davies wrote to her friend Miss Richardson:

My Dear Anna,

We are here. The little band arrived in due succession on Saturday, and we have now had three lectures. . . . Adelaide [Miss Manning] has just been ejaculating "It *is* so pleasant to be at the College", and the students are saying it in their bright faces and in their tones all day. I scarcely expected that they could all have worked together with such entire cordiality and that so small a number could be so "jolly". Miss Lloyd is most valuable. Being a little older than the others, she makes a link between them and the authorities. . . . Miss Lloyd is a little behind the rest both in Latin and Mathematics, and incessantly proclaims her despair of doing anything. She sends you a message that she doubts whether she will live till Christmas, but whatever happens, she will stick to it till she dies. Mr Clark's teaching of Latin is most interesting. . . . They say Mr Stuart's explanations of Mathematics are exceedingly clear. . . . I find a great deal of time goes in talking with the students. They come here by ones and twos and we get into talks. Mrs Manning is delighted with their faces, and wants to have photographs of them all. We are pretty civilized now and quite comfortable. We have good plain food, milk, bread, beef, and mutton, and it disappears very fast. The fresh pure air, and perhaps also being in good spirits, gives everybody an appetite. . . . Mrs Austin undertook the worst of the furnishing and settling and did it admirably, but it is not quite finished yet.

Benslow House, as Miss Davies said, had a foundation of plainness and solidity, and it was beautifully placed on a chalk cliff above Hitchin, with wide views over Hertfordshire. The garden was large and pleasant, with flower borders and shrubberies, and it was shaded with well-grown trees. One room served both as bedroom and sitting room for each student, except two, who had, as well as a bedroom apiece, a small study—in one case a converted china closet. Miss Davies was not to reside at the College, but she would have to pay at least one official visit at the beginning of each term, to arrange about lectures, and a room was therefore set apart for her. A room on the ground floor, known as "the Library", served both as a common room for the students, and as a lecture room. In the basement was what Miss Davies called "the dining-hall". Everything was planned by her in detail, and with careful regard to the dignity and correctness befitting a College. "The plan proposed", she wrote to Mrs Manning, "is a students' table and a Mistress's table, the first long and narrow, to sit only on one side, with their faces towards the Mistress's table, the other a rather small oval, for the Mistress and the Supernumerary [Miss Manning], and (if invited) the Sec. [Miss Davies herself]." Miss Lumsden has described the students' view of these arrangements:

The dining-room was in the basement, a bare ugly room with two tables, at one end of which we students sat, while the Mistress and her friends sat at the "High table" alongside. It was at first expected that we should sit in a formal row down one side of our table, lest we should be guilty of the discourtesy of turning our backs upon the "High". But this was too much, and we rebelled. Conversation cannot but flag if people have to sit in a row, and we quietly ignored rule and insisted upon comfortably facing each other. So academically formal . . . was the order imposed from the first at Hitchin—we might have been fifty undergraduates instead of five harmless young women.[1]

Beneath this formality there lay a definite purpose. Miss Davies was determined that the College should be a real College, and not a new variety of girls' school;

[1] "The Ancient History of Girton College", by Miss L. I. Lumsden, *Girton Review*, Michaelmas Term, 1907.

she wanted everything to be done from the very beginning with due regard to dignity and decorum.
Down to the smallest detail, she felt that all they did
was of historic importance, and that the lines which
future generations were to follow must be rightly laid
down. This feeling was understood and shared by the
students. "It needed an effort of imagination", writes
Miss Gibson, "to recognize Dons and high table and
undergraduates all complete, though as it were in
embryo: but it was an effort that Miss Davies was
fully prepared to make and to insist upon. Just at
first she did not need to insist, for there was not one
of these five first-comers who was not weighted with
a sense of responsibility for the new start. They were
all much on their guard against being treated as
school-girls, and in the case of three, at least, out of
the five, age alone was not enough to differentiate
them."

The students were very various in age, experience,
and attainments. Miss Townshend, the youngest
daughter of an English family resident in Ireland
since the time of Cromwell, was a quick-witted, clever,
and sensitive girl, a great admirer of William Morris
and the Pre-Raphaelites, and her "aesthetic" en-
thusiasms brought a novel element into the little
circle. Miss Lloyd, in particular, used in after years
to say that her fellow-students had opened her eyes
about art, and that she had learned from them that
it was one of the foundations of happiness. "Miss
Woodhead, the youngest, aged eighteen," writes
Miss Gibson, "had only recently left a good Quaker

school, but had already begun teaching: Miss Lloyd was older than any of us, a woman of culture, and also a Friend. She did not come with the intention of reading for a degree examination, but for a quiet time of leisure and study. Her presence was valuable as a mellowing influence. This was even more true of the gracious and charming lady who was our Mistress during the first term. Mrs Manning was frail and elderly, and one cannot wonder that she felt unable to occupy the post permanently, but we all regretted her leaving us, and felt that we had lost a friend. The College has never had a more suitable and dignified Head than during its first term. Her suavity and gentle courtesy complemented perfectly Miss Davies's eager abrupt decisiveness."

With the Lent Term, there came a new student—Miss Rachel Cook, who had previously been kept away by illness. Miss Cook's character and personality were such as to make a great impression on her fellow-students. "Her presence made itself felt the moment she entered the room", writes Miss Gibson. "It is impossible to convey an impression of her charm by any inventory of her features, but no man or woman ever failed to feel it. George Eliot once described her as nymphlike.... One did not need to wait for the delicate staccato idiom of her speech to decide that her romantic type of beauty could belong only to Highland blood." Miss Maynard, who entered the College two years later, has also described some of the first generation of students. Miss Cook was "beautiful in face as in mind, and had the endowment of that scholarly instinct that industry alone can never attain.... Her father had been Professor of Moral Philosophy at St Andrews, and she had been brought up in the atmosphere of a University, as none of the rest of us had been". Miss Woodhead was "a stalwart north-country girl with an erect figure and a fine pair of shoulders...more given to long walks and to gathering branches of trees than to any sort of literary interest". Miss Woodhead and Miss Gibson read mathematics, Miss Cook and Miss Lumsden classics. Of the last named Miss Maynard writes: "We all...looked upon her not only as the senior student, but as our true head and representative. In her we saw the life of the College at its intensest and most glowing point, for there we found the widest sympathies, the highest aspirations, the severest struggles.... She appreciated the new outlook in a wider and more sagacious manner than any one of the rest of us at the time.... It would be hard to tell the gain to any one of us, and a definite part of that gain was her gift".[1]

Someone said that the students were "the happiest women in England". Miss Lumsden, on being asked, during her first term at Hitchin, what was the uppermost feeling in her mind, answered, "Gladness". She had had a free and happy life at home; but country pursuits and travel both at home and abroad had not satisfied her. Hitchin brought the one thing that had been lacking in her life—aim. Miss Maynard had similar experiences. She first heard of the College

[1] *Between College Terms*, by C. L. Maynard.

from a sister of Miss Cook, who was able to describe it exactly. "The whole was a new world to me," Miss Maynard writes, "yet even while she was speaking, a conviction came to me, '*That's* what you have been waiting for!'. . . The extraordinary happiness of that first year at Hitchin is a thing that cannot come twice in a lifetime. . . . I was. . . adopted at once by R. Cook and L. I. Lumsden, and I need hardly say they opened a new world of thought to me." Miss Maynard has recorded elsewhere that she used to wake every morning in her first term or two "with a sort of sting of delight, and think, 'Here is a whole day more at College!'"

The life at Hitchin was on the whole a very quiet and studious one. For recreation, besides country walks and the Hitchin swimming bath, the students had croquet, and Mr Tomkinson taught them also to play fives, as Dame Louisa Lumsden tells us, "with great laughter and fun, but with small success from the point of view of the game". Miss Davies learned fives with the rest, and enjoyed herself thoroughly. "I am cheered by hearing that the beginning of Hitchin looks so happy and promising", wrote George Eliot to her; "I care so much about individual happiness that I think it is a great thing to work for, only to make half-a-dozen lives rather better than they might otherwise be."

As the first term drew to a close, the problem of finding a Mistress in succession to Mrs Manning became urgent. It was solved by the appointment of Miss Emily Shirreff, a lady who had long been interested in the problem of women's education, and had written a book upon the subject. "She has a Stoical way of talking which attracts me", wrote Miss Davies to her friend Miss Richardson. "Her view of coming here is simply that if she is wanted, and can do it, she ought. She takes a modest view of her duties, and undertakes them simply, without any grand air of self-sacrifice. It is a spirited thing to do, from mere interest in the idea, at her age. She is I believe about 55, ladylike and gentle in manner, and I fancy a good deal of a student.... We are to have Miss Wedgwood also next Term. The students think it would enable them to get on faster with Classics if they had some help from a resident Tutor, so Miss W. has kindly consented to come for a month, as an experiment. The difficulty in the way is her deafness. We can only find out by trying whether that is too great a drawback.... To have a person of her noble nature and keen interest in study is worth sacrificing a good deal for."

Miss Shirreff took up the duties of the Mistress in the Lent Term of 1870. Miss Gibson remembers her as "elderly, beautiful, and beautifully dressed, of the fine-lady type, a contrast to the plain-speaking and downright manners of Miss Davies and Lady Stanley of Alderley. She was full of reminiscences and talked in an interesting way about the distinguished people she had known—Buckle,[1] for instance, to whom she had been engaged". The new Mistress, for her part, was delighted with the students. "Miss Shirreff is as

[1] Author of *The History of Civilization in England.*

much struck as Mrs Manning was by the elevation of their talk", wrote Miss Davies to Miss Manning. Miss Richardson, who visited the College in the following year, thought "the whole life of the students looked only *too* intellectually luxurious; but they are a remarkably interesting set of young women".

The intellectual luxury was, however, not so great as it seemed to Miss Richardson. "Our teaching during the first year was scanty but excellent", writes Miss Gibson. "We should no doubt have been better in those early days for a little more advice and teaching. Our lecturers came once or twice a week, and there was no one to appeal to in between. Miss Julia Wedgwood stood in the gap for a time. I do not know that her classical teaching was of great assistance, but she was an interesting and delightful personality, and enriched the life of our little community." "Four lecturers came to Hitchin in the first term, Messrs Seeley, Hort, Clark and Stuart," writes Dame Louisa Lumsden, "and we had one lecture every day which everybody attended, the length of this lecture being fixed neither by our capacities of taking in knowledge, nor by the convenience of the lecturer, but by the hours of railway trains. The only exception to this rule was Mr Hort, as he came from the neighbouring rectory of St Ippolyt's, therefore his lecture lasted only the reasonable time of one hour." Mr E. C. Clark came twice a week from Cambridge for both Latin and Greek. Miss Gibson describes the work as "very elementary, for we were all beginners, but the class was small and eager, and Mr Clark the most patient, painstaking and thorough of teachers, so that we got on pretty quickly and enjoyed the lectures immensely....For a single term we had lectures on English from Mr Seeley. This had been looked forward to as a signal honour and great opportunity, for *Ecce Homo* was to many of us the book of the day, but the lectures were disappointing. Seeley was not a born teacher; dry, critical, and sarcastic, he demanded bricks without straw".

Professor Seeley, as we have seen, despised the Cambridge course, and instead of keeping to the subjects required for it, he lectured on *Lvcidas*, and set the students to write original verse; Dr Hort likewise lectured on the Acts, though St Luke's Gospel was the set book for the Little-go; Mr Clark alone took a practical view of the position and kept strictly to the Little-go subjects. "By this, as well as by his most interesting and stimulating teaching, he earned our warmest gratitude", writes Dame Louisa Lumsden. Next term an additional classical lecturer was appointed, Mr C. E. Graves. "No words", writes Dame Louisa, "are enough to do justice to the services of Mr Clark and Mr Graves." Mr Stuart, the mathematical lecturer (afterwards Professor of Mechanics at Cambridge), was a little later succeeded by Mr J. F. Moulton,[1] fresh from his honours as Senior Wrangler and Smith's Prizeman. "He poured an amazing illumination on elementary mathematics" for Miss Gibson and Miss Woodhead. They found

[1] Afterwards Lord Justice Moulton.

the work a severe struggle, but were urged on by Miss Davies.

Miss Gibson, however, was lured away by a growing interest in other matters. "As soon as opportunity offered for a wider choice of subjects", she writes, "my allegiance wavered. I had already begun to take an interest in Political Economy, and when Mr Venn's lectures began in my third year, I spent a good deal of time in reading for them, and was much thrilled to find at the end of it that we were to be examined by my saint and hero, the author of *The Subjection of Women*.[1]...Perhaps if one had gone up straight from school, one would have been inured to the restraint of reading with an examination ahead, but the definite goal grew more and more unattractive to me as time went on. I always wanted to spend my time on the wrong things, and when I found that the last term must be spent in revising tiresome elementary work, I made up my mind not to stay for it."

Want of preparation made the burden of the examinations very heavy. The long pull of elementary work to pass the Little-go and the additional subjects (all mathematics) was, as Miss Maynard recalls, a very great strain, and with some of the students two years had to be spent upon this before they could enter (well tired out) on the Tripos work, with barely four terms at their disposal. "No allowance whatever was made for our colossal ignorance of the special subjects required....Three years and one term was

[1] The papers set for the students by J. S. Mill are to be found in his *Letters*, vol. II, p. 336.

in those days the time allowed to men in which to take the Tripos, and Miss Emily Davies scorned all compromises and her students must conform to the same rule."[1] The students were there for the College, not the College for the students. To Miss Davies the individual, as Dame Louisa Lumsden has said, was "a mere cog in the wheel of her great scheme. There was a fine element in this, a total indifference to popularity, but...it was plain that we counted for little or nothing, except as we furthered her plans".

Among other members of the Committee, Mr Bryce was the one who took most interest in the students' work. He visited the College several times, gave a few lectures on Greek history, and invited the students to write essays during the vacation for him to criticize. On one occasion he paid an unexpected visit, and, as Dame Louisa Lumsden relates, "unfortunately only one student was in, Miss Townshend. On our return from a long walk, we were greatly amused by her description of her interview with the visitor. 'You see', said she to him, 'nobody here knows anything!' It was a startling criticism of Hitchin arrangements". And it was true—no one at Benslow House could be guided by experience. The ladies on the Committee were not familiar with University work, and did not realize the task set before the students. The lecturers had never before had pupils quite like these, mature, intelligent, and eager to learn, but wonderfully ignorant; and they found it difficult to enter seriously into the plan of preparing

[1] *Between College Terms,* by C. L. Maynard.

them for the Honours examinations. The students had to grope for what they needed. Though they felt the kindness of Professor Seeley and Mr Hort, they were forced into the ungracious position of having to rebel and demand to be taught the subjects essential for their purpose. In a conversation with Professor Seeley they explained that they wished to give up his classes owing to the necessity of spending all their time on examination subjects. This was more than he could bear, and he resigned his place on the Executive Committee. "It seems to me a great misfortune", he wrote to Miss Davies, "that the College should seem to the outer world, just at this critical time, to be nothing but a reproduction of Cambridge with all its faults.... Just at the moment when education is taking a new shape I cannot take any pleasure in attending to the details of a College where the old and to me obsolete routine goes on....I cannot do more than passively wish you well....I do not feel prepared to give my time to you." Other lecturers were appointed on the staff; and the students helped each other, Miss Lumsden, Miss Woodhead, and Miss Gibson adding to their own work by coaching others in the Little-go subjects.

Difficulties as to the work and the teaching naturally made themselves felt in the second term, as the students began to find out what the work really meant. There were other troubles as well. Complaints as to the food seem to show that the housekeeping was perhaps too economical, and some details of discipline proved irksome to the students. Certain points, such as having to ask leave of absence from morning service on Sundays, and the presence of chaperones at lectures, were waived by Miss Shirreff. The rule that the gates must be closed at a certain hour was disliked by some of the students, who did not know that this was usual in a College. There was no custom or tradition to guide them or the authorities in their relation to each other. Miss Shirreff was the constituted resident authority, but Miss Davies was felt to be the real though not official head. "In spirit she was continually with us," writes Dame Louisa Lumsden, "and her will was felt to be the driving force throughout." "I have had a little talk with Miss Lumsden about the life here", wrote Miss Davies to Miss Manning. "She says it is not amusement that they want, but *interests*, and I believe it is so. They want to *feel* the links between the large outer world and their own work, not to be distracted from it." The isolation at Hitchin and the extreme smallness of the community were in fact beginning to be felt by the students. But their interest was still keen in the new life and in each other, and they used to sit up at night discussing everything in heaven and earth. Miss Lloyd, who was obliged to leave before long owing to the demands of her family, often said afterwards that the short time she had spent at the College was full of stimulus and inspiration, and that what she had absorbed there was a source of joy through the rest of her life.

MISS DAVIES *to* MISS ANNA RICHARDSON

June 23 [1870]

The old students—they begin to grow venerable—separated in a pleasant state of mind; I had a talk with them the evening I left on the results of one year, putting it in the form of the question whether it would be worth while to come for a year only. The thing Miss Lloyd feels to have gained is some appreciation of the scholarly, as distinguished from the man-of-business way of looking at things. Miss Lumsden said that before she came, she used to feel fearfully solitary. She was always having said to her, "Oh, but you're so exceptional". Now, she feels herself belonging to a body, and has lost the sense of loneliness. Miss Townshend has learnt that she does not know how to study. Before she came, she thought she did. Also, she feels it a relief to have taken a step, from which she could not go back even if she wished. She has got rid of the harass of the daily self-questioning about what she had better do with herself. Miss Gibson replied briefly that one year was much better than nothing. Miss Cook said she would rather not come at all than that, and being asked why, explained that it was because she would be so sorry to go away. Miss Gibson said she should feel that just as much at the end of the three years, to which there was a chorus of assent. Miss Woodhead answered my question with an emphatic "Oh, I should think it *quite* worth while". I asked what was the good of it and she replied with a still more emphatic *Oh!*—which remains unexplained, as my train would not wait. You will understand that we were not talking about the amount of *learning* to be gained. I do not wonder that they like being at the College for the sake of each other's company. They are delightful to live with. I only hope the new set may turn out as nice.

Miss Shirreff's appointment had never been regarded as permanent, either by herself or by the Committee. She retired after two terms, and the difficulty of finding a Mistress had again to be faced. "Mrs Gurney thinks", wrote Miss Davies to Mrs Manning, "the *best* thing would be to have a transcendently fit person (such as Lady Rich) who could be entirely trusted on all points. But in the absence of this transcendent person—who is not likely to be found by advertising or by 'looking out', the next best thing is to have some one like Mrs Austin, whom we know well and could trust thoroughly as to the most essential things." Mrs Austin was a gentle, amiable woman, with some sense of humour, most conscientious and willing in all she undertook, and always ready to befriend the students in illness or trouble. She had not, however, the wide intellectual outlook of Mrs Manning, and she was not strong in health, and inclined to be over-anxious. Naturally she leaned much upon Miss Davies, whom she consulted constantly, even as to small details of housekeeping and discipline. The task was growing. Three new students[1] came in October, 1870, and as the house could not hold them all, a long iron building was set up in the orchard, and divided by curtains into small rooms. "Even the present small increase of number is working advantageously as to the Lectures", Miss Davies wrote to Miss Richardson. "It enables us to have more of them, and shorter hours at a time. The new Lecturers are much liked.

[1] Miss Gamble, Miss Slade, and Miss Tidman.

The new rooms also (we call them the Tabernacle—
in the wilderness, on the way to the Promised Land)
have turned out pretty and comfortable. And the old
and new students work in together pleasantly."

Miss Davies viewed the Tabernacle through rose-
coloured spectacles. "Life in the tin house", writes
Dame Louisa Lumsden, "was a misery. If it rained,
the rattle on the roof was maddening; if the sun shone
we were baked as in an oven; and the rooms were
so small that Miss Woodhead, a tall athletic young
woman, declared that in her doll's house sitting room,
without rising from her chair, by merely reaching out
a long arm she could either poke the fire or open the
door." Miss Kingsland (now Mrs Higgs) relates that
she could hear the scratch of her neighbour's pen as
she sat at work. Mice gambolled between the tin
walls and the paper with which they were lined, and
the nightingales in the orchard added more pleasantly,
but quite as noisily, to the disturbance.

As the number of students increased, things became more lively, and it was possible to have dancing
in the evenings, as well as debates, Shakespeare
readings, and so forth. Miss Davies attended these
functions as an onlooker, and generally took a quiet
and rather reserved part in all that was going on.
Beneath a surface of quiet decorum, she enjoyed life
at Hitchin intensely. "A mere sight of the students",
she wrote to Miss Richardson, "does not convey any
adequate sense of the delightfulness of living among
them." A good many varieties of religious opinion
were represented in the College. Some of the students

went to a Congregational Chapel, some to the services at the Parish Church, or to Dr Hort's services at St Ippolyt's, where among the congregation were to be seen old labourers dressed in smocks, standing during the sermon. Miss Davies put no pressure on anyone to go to Church. All were left free to do as they chose, and though differences of religious opinion made themselves felt, the strong College spirit which ruled from the first helped them, as a student of that time has said, "to shake down together".

In the October Term of 1870 came a great event in the life of the College—the Little-go. Despised as it was, this examination was regarded by Miss Davies and the students as the first touchstone on which to prove their worth. Every step in the process was a crisis. Application had first to be made to the University authorities for leave for the students to take the papers, and a refusal would have demolished the whole object of their first year's work. When the answer came from the Council of the Senate, it was to the effect that it was not within their province to give the permission asked for, but that there would be no objection to a private arrangement being made with the examiners. Miss Davies accordingly wrote to the Senior Examiner, Mr Cartmell, asking him to take the matter into his hands, and make what arrangements seemed right with the other examiners. The examiners consented to undertake the work, and the five second-year students prepared themselves to face the ordeal at the end of the October Term. Dame Louisa Lumsden describes her experiences as follows:

We went up to Cambridge for it, and Miss Davies did me a good turn, for she kindly introduced me to a countrywoman of my own, Mrs Latham, a most kind and charming woman whose guest I became. With her I saw Cambridge under delightful guidance. We lunched, for instance, at Queens', and I recollect how kind old Dr Phillips, the President, froze my blood by innocently remarking, in his slow and somewhat pompous fashion, that he believed there were "some young women up in Cambridge to pass the Little-go!"

"Yes," said Mrs Latham coolly, "and there sits one." I could have sunk under the table! But both Dr and Mrs Phillips were so kind, and they took the terrible revelation so calmly, that I was soon reassured.

Not so, however, did it fare with me at Jesus College. Before we ventured into these once conventual precincts, Mrs Latham warned me on no account to divulge the secret of my quest at Cambridge; the result might, she said, be that I might find myself summarily ejected from the house. Nothing was farther from my desires than to be either a martyr or a nine days' wonder, and I need hardly say that I kept a discreet silence.

The success of the Hitchin candidates was recorded by *Punch* as an entertaining novelty. All the five passed in classics, and two (Miss Gibson and Miss Woodhead) passed also in the additional mathematical subjects. Not till the Michaelmas Term of 1871 were the other three (Miss Townshend, Miss Cook and Miss Lumsden) ready for the additionals. The Senior Examiner declined to examine them, but happily Mr Cartmell was one of the examiners for the year, and he consented to look over their papers. Dame Louisa's account may again be quoted:

There still remained for my torment the Additional Mathematical Subjects—to me an almost insuperable barrier. Was ever anybody, I thought, so hopelessly stupid at Mathematics as I? The only resource was to devote all my energies to them, and I gave up Classics entirely.

You can imagine perhaps what it cost me to take such a step as this in my third year. However, my plan answered, and I got through in the Additionals, whereas Miss Townshend, who had no difficulty in Mathematics, but had not cut down her other work for their sake, failed, and gave up the Tripos altogether. It was no doubt the only wise thing to do at that late stage, but it was a great disappointment to us all. To Miss Woodhead and Miss Gibson, who were endlessly patient with my Mathematical deficiencies, I owe my success. For a sort of mutual help society had existed among us from the first, and thus to some extent we supplied gaps in teaching by coaching one another.

It was a difficult and anxious business for inexperienced people to work for a Tripos, hampered up to the last moment by the Little-go, and by doubts not only as to whether they would pass, but even as to whether they would be allowed to try. Relief was needed from the strain, and the students felt the want of interests and recreations, not easily supplied in such a small community. This led to an episode which illustrates the difficulties encountered by those who had to work out a system of College life and discipline, on the smallest possible scale with the scantiest materials, and without previous experience of anything of the kind. As Miss Gibson relates, it nearly caused a catastrophe "owing to Miss Davies's somewhat exaggerated anxiety about the proprieties and our equally exaggerated jealousy with regard to the rights, privileges, and liberty of students". Her story continues:

Our number by this time was almost doubled, and we had become perhaps a little less earnest about our work, the Little-go being behind us, and a little more enterprising about amusements. There was an institution which had been started during the first term, called "The College Five". It held weekly evening meetings for reading and discussion of a more or less formal kind. This little club now aspired to run a small dramatic entertainment. We were bold enough to undertake to act a number of selected scenes from Shakespeare. Of course we wanted to make the performance as realistic as possible, and various stage properties were invented or procured.... When all was ready, we decided to invite the Dons, Miss Davies, Miss Wedgwood and Mrs Austin, and also the servants, to witness a dress rehearsal in the common room....

We, the actors, were painfully conscious during the performance that our efforts were not being well received, and after it was over, the storm broke. Our men's clothes were a scandal and the whole performance an outrage on the proprieties which might prove fatal to the future of the College.

The hot-heads among us took umbrage and disputed, with distant politeness, the right of the College authorities to interfere in such matters. Relations with Miss Davies became strained, and the upshot was that the College Committee was to be summoned to discuss the whole affair, and we were requested in the meantime not to proceed with the performance.

It was an absurd instance of making mountains out of molehills, and I am afraid I was one of the worst offenders, for I remember that I and one or two others seriously considered whether we ought not to play the part of the village Hampden, and leave the College as a protest against tyranny.

The affair caused Miss Davies much anxiety, but the catastrophe was fortunately averted. "To me", writes Miss Gibson, "the most important outcome of the imbroglio was an interview with Madame Bodichon who was deputed...to pay me a domiciliary visit, and reason with me with reference not only to my rôle as ringleader in the theatrical revolt, but to the style of dress which I was beginning to affect. With regard to the latter I scored. It happened that I had recently gone into mourning and, as a protest against the hideous and fussy fashions of the time, I had contrived a simple little frock of fine paramatta not unlike the coat-frocks of to-day....It was jeered at, at home, as my 'preacher's gown', but when Madame Bodichon found me in it in my room at Hitchin she was charmed with it. It was a case of the prophet coming to curse and remaining to bless, for she asked me for the pattern and said she would have a gown made like it to paint in."

Out of the difficulty arose a friendship, a not uncommon experience in such matters. The question of acting was never formally discussed by the Committee; the performance was dropped, and no more said. On the other hand, no difficulties were raised when at Girton a dramatic club was started, only a few years later. At the moment, Miss Davies was greatly relieved. In a memorandum written long afterwards, she notes: "It seemed at the moment as if the existence of the College was at stake, as while it was felt to be impossible to allow the practice, the withdrawal of some of the students might have been ruinous".

The incident made it clear to Miss Davies that the students really needed something in the way of outside interests. The Hitchin students felt this the more because they were not the products of school routine. Their previous experience of life made them feel the College in some ways a restriction, and not an enlargement of interests. Nevertheless they had something which is perhaps lacking in the full-grown Girton of to-day. The infant College had something of the child's zest in life, when the most ordinary things are new discoveries, and every day brings adventures. The spontaneous gaiety and happiness, in which Miss Davies took such delight, were like an overflow when some barrier has been burst. The students revelled in newly found intellectual interests, and in a novel and delightful relation with each other; the thrill of a new movement, as Miss Gibson has said, gave comradeship to their intercourse. And they knew that upon their success it would depend whether others would be able to follow after them. They had the stimulus (new to women) of feeling that much was expected of them, and they rose gallantly to the occasion. There were of course moments of discontent and disappointment, but the whole thing was an adventure, and a mixture, as all great adventures should be, of the highest spirits with the most intense determination. Experiences such as these cannot last, and cannot be repeated.

CHAPTER IV

FROM HITCHIN TO GIRTON

A dangerous rival. Financial struggles. Decision to build at Girton. Miss Davies appointed Mistress. The Girton Pioneers. The new buildings. Relations with Cambridge. Internal difficulties. Miss Davies's retirement from the Mistress-ship.

WHILE the great experiment was being carried on at Hitchin, the Examinations for Women established in 1869 had already led to further developments in the direction feared by Miss Davies. In the autumn of that year, Mr Sidgwick, Mrs Fawcett and others took steps to organize lectures for women in Cambridge, in connection with the examinations. The lectures began in the Lent Term of 1870, and had an immediate success, being attended by nearly eighty ladies, residents in Cambridge. Students from a distance were soon attracted by the lectures, and by scholarships offered in connection with the examinations. The lectures were organized on a more permanent basis through the formation of the Association for Promoting the Higher Education of Women in Cambridge; and it soon became evident that a house of residence for women students was wanted.

Meanwhile the number of students at Hitchin was increasing, and the question of house room had become urgent. The lease of Benslow House was due to expire at Michaelmas, 1872, and it was necessary to decide where the permanent home of the College was to be. Mr Sidgwick, who, as we have seen, was a member of the Cambridge Committee, thought that the College and the Association for Promoting the Higher Education of Women in Cambridge might very well join forces in order to provide what they both needed—a house of residence for women students in Cambridge. Miss Davies, however, declined all co-operation. Nothing would induce her to do anything to support the Association, since it was engaged in forwarding a scheme of education specially designed for women. She was, moreover, determined that the College should not be placed in Cambridge, though she found some difficulty in stating her reasons for this. "The advantages", she wrote to Mr Sidgwick, "are obvious and tangible; the objections are more subtle and difficult to put into words without making them look foolish." She argued the case with him in a long letter, the gist of which was, that if the College were in Cambridge, social claims would render the students liable to such frequent interruption as to make it very difficult for them to work seriously; there would be "a decrease in the eager receptiveness of the students and possibly also a lower standard of health". To her friend Miss Richardson she explained candidly what she could not bring herself to say to Mr Sidgwick:

We have been asked with hands held up in horror, were we going to Cambridge?...Young women are kept away now by parental fears. Their mothers would let them come if it was considered a creditable thing to do. Ladies of influence have to make other people think it creditable. It takes a good deal of zeal and courage to speak of the College as it is. If the more extreme course were adopted, a whole system of propaganda would be stopped. People like Mrs Gurney and Lady Augusta would feel their mouths closed. As Mrs Gurney said, they would be almost ashamed to speak of it....We had two visits from brothers at Hitchin, and tho' everybody concerned behaved with the utmost propriety, we felt thankful that brothers did not live within thirty miles.

Mr Sidgwick did his best to persuade Miss Davies, and the Cambridge Committee unanimously expressed their opinion that it would be far best for the College to be established in Cambridge. "The moral objections", wrote Mr Sedley Taylor, "seem to be imaginary." Madame Bodichon too was in favour of Cambridge. But all was in vain, and Miss Davies carried her point. A compromise between Cambridge and Hitchin, favoured by Mr Tomkinson, was finally adopted, and it was determined to build near, but not in, Cambridge. The Cambridge Committee, their unanimous advice having been disregarded, felt that there was no more need for them, and their meetings were discontinued. Their Secretary, Mr Sedley Taylor, remained on the Executive Committee and took an active part in the search which now began for a building site near Cambridge.

Mr Sidgwick, who was thoroughly in earnest, was not to be defeated in his plans, and he immediately set about the establishment of a house of residence in Cambridge. But difficulties now arose with his Committee, who, though they wanted to facilitate girls coming to Cambridge to attend lectures, did not want to be responsible for them. Mr Sidgwick courageously decided to take the responsibility himself, and to open a house for students as a separate enterprise. He asked Miss A. J. Clough to take charge, and the house was opened in the Michaelmas Term, 1871, at 74 Regent Street, Cambridge, with five students. The venture grew and prospered, and in course of time became Newnham College.

It must have seemed at the moment very regrettable that Miss Davies and Mr Sidgwick could not agree to amalgamate their schemes. The disagreement, however, proved fortunate, as it led to the foundation of two Colleges instead of one. The two have been most helpful to each other, each supplying its own element of usefulness in the development of women's education at Cambridge. As time went by, the essential causes of difference disappeared, and they now act in close co-operation as regards Entrance Scholarship Examinations and other matters. In the beginning, however, they were to some extent in antagonism to each other, and it was very doubtful whether the friends of women's education were numerous and rich enough to make it possible for both to survive. Mr Sidgwick's scheme had arisen within Cambridge, and had all the advantages of his influence in the University, and of a curriculum adapted to what were thought to be the special needs of women. Miss Davies had lost the support of the Cambridge Committee, and her position was full of difficulties. For a moment she almost felt that the

College would have to go under, but, as she wrote to Mr Sidgwick, "We are not going to give in yet".

Want of funds was one of the greatest obstacles. The initial sum aimed at was £30,000; but it proved difficult to scrape together even so much as £7000. After a vigorous campaign of meetings, the total was brought up to £7200. The Building Committee cut down the plans as far as possible, going so far as to dispense with a library for the sake of saving £650, but with all their efforts, there was not enough money to justify their entering into a building contract. It was decided to borrow money on the security of a number of guarantors, and to make this possible the College had to be brought into legal existence. It was accordingly incorporated as an Association under the Board of Trade. A governing body was created, consisting of thirty "Members of the College", including all those who had been on the Executive Committee, except Mrs Manning (who died in 1871), Professor Seeley, and Mr Hastings; with, in addition, Lady Stanley of Alderley, Lady Rich (a cousin of Mr Tomkinson), Mrs Ponsonby, Mr F. Seebohm of Hitchin, Mr James Bryce, and Miss Shirreff. Most of the business continued to be carried on by the Executive Committee, which was elected by the Members of the College. There were to be six Representative Members—three to be elected by the Cambridge Senate, if and when it should choose to recognize the College, and three by the future Certificated Students of the College. The Certificated Students were to correspond to graduates, and would receive a certificate from the College setting forth that they had fulfilled all the conditions necessary for a Cambridge degree.

After much search, a building site of sixteen acres was bought, near the junction of the Girton and Huntingdon roads, almost a mile and a half northwest of Cambridge. As the new building could not be ready in time for the October Term of 1872, it was arranged for the students to remain in their restricted quarters at Hitchin for one more year.

Meanwhile, in the spring of 1872, Mrs Austin's health had broken down, and she was obliged to leave suddenly in the middle of the Lent Term. Miss Davies went at once to Hitchin, but she could not stay long, and for the remainder of the term her place was taken in turn by Madame Bodichon and Lady Stanley of Alderley—two most unacademic people. At this critical moment, with the move to Cambridge in prospect, it was of great importance that the Mistress-ship should be held by someone who could be completely trusted to guide the College aright. Miss Davies, as Secretary, had hitherto kept the arrangements as to lectures and studies in her own hands; but with the growth of the College this was becoming more difficult for a non-resident official. The Mistress's duties were deficient in interest and importance because they did not include this part of the work, and so long as this was the case, it would be difficult to induce any highly qualified woman to accept the post. Yet Miss Davies was very unwilling to let these arrangements slip out of her hands; her experiences with the "evil principle" had made her too anxious. "If the charge of the studies were to be given over to the Mistress, it would be giving up everything", she wrote to Mr Tomkinson, the one of all her colleagues whose opinion she respected most. "Nothing but the impossibility of getting a really fit person would bring me to consent to my own appointment." But she was, as Mrs Gurney said, "*driven into being Mistress at last*". While retaining the post of Secretary, she took up her duties as Mistress at Michaelmas, 1872, and settled down at Hitchin with thirteen students.

And now a new crisis, a climax in the affairs of the College, claimed attention. Three students were ready to take Triposes—Miss Woodhead in mathematics, Miss Cook and Miss Lumsden in classics. An ally appeared in the person of Mr Gunson, of Christ's College, who wished to propose a Grace authorizing examiners in all University examinations to admit students of Girton College. The Grace was rejected by the Council of the Senate by 10 votes to 6. Fortunately, the Council, as Mr Gunson wrote, "carefully abstained from expressing any disapproval of our Examiners examining your students in their private capacity and in a clandestine way". Miss Davies accordingly applied to the examiners for "the favour of their assistance", and though they were not all willing to act, a sufficient number consented to look over the papers "in their private capacity, and without the slightest reference to their office as University Examiners". These correspondences had to be renewed annually till the position was regularized by the Senate in 1881. Every year the same anxieties had to be gone through. A total refusal was always possible and would have been disastrous, but happily there were always enough examiners willing to act.

The three Tripos candidates were chaperoned by Miss Davies to Cambridge, where they took the examination in their sitting room at the University Arms. The messenger with the papers was an hour late, having been sent to the wrong address, and Miss Davies and the candidates suffered torments of anxiety, fearing that the examiners had declined after all to act. In the end, however, all was well, and the three candidates passed triumphantly. When the great news arrived at Hitchin, the students climbed on to the roof and rang the alarm bell with such effect that the Hitchin police began to get out the fire engine. When the Mistress remonstrated, they fell back on singing *Gaudeamus igitur*, and tying three flags to the chimneys. Their rejoicings were well justified, for a great point had been gained. At a time when women's power to make any serious effort was very generally denied, and doubt was felt as to girls' capacity for profiting by good teaching, it was of great value to demonstrate that women could pass University examinations in Honours, under the same conditions as those imposed on men.

But the conditions, though nominally the same, pressed much more hardly upon women students, owing to their lack of previous preparation. They had to learn their Tripos subjects almost from the beginning, and yet had to give up precious time to preparing for the Little-go, almost till the moment of the Tripos itself. It is hardly surprising to find that a rebellion was organized among the students, who all joined in sending a petition to the Executive Committee, asking that students should be allowed to become candidates for Triposes without passing the Little-go. Seven of the Cambridge men who lectured at the College supported them. The petition (which, it need hardly be said, was not granted) caused great distress to Miss Davies, as it cut at the root of all that she was fighting for. To have special indulgences granted to women would, she felt, defeat the great object she had in view—their full and free admission to the best education of the time. The temporary sacrifice of obliging a few women students to take Latin and Greek papers for which their previous education had not prepared them was in her eyes well worth while for the sake of the cause; and the students had hitherto responded with such wonderful spirit and success that the sacrifice perhaps did not seem to her a very serious one. Most of the students accepted their defeat loyally, and gradually came to a better understanding of her point of view. "Miss Davies was right", wrote Miss Lumsden many years afterwards. "Even then I felt it. I am heartily glad she carried her point. That sacrifice of the individual was thoroughly worth while."

Meanwhile the College was being built at Girton. These first buildings comprised the small block now

forming that side of the Emily Davies Court which
includes the old front door and the clock (which was
put up in 1873 in memory of Mrs Manning, the first
Mistress). There were rooms for twenty-one students,
the Mistress (hers were the rooms on the first floor,
under the clock),[1] one resident lecturer, three lecture
rooms, and a small dining hall,[2] including a bow
window for which £50 was given by Lady Stanley.
Funds were not enough to build a library or a laboratory. In spite of the financial difficulties, Miss Davies
was determined that the thing should be well done.
Mr Alfred Waterhouse, one of the foremost architects
of the time, made the plans in close consultation with
her, and it is remarkable that the later parts of the
building show no alteration in scale. From the beginning it was planned that the students should, as
far as possible, have a bedroom and sitting room
apiece, and the corridors are as wide in the oldest part
of the building as in the newest—a striking testimony
to Miss Davies's forethought, and to her faith in the
success of the College—a faith which to many must
have seemed foolhardy, especially considering the
official attitude of the University.[3] By September,

[1] The tiles in the fireplace are from designs by Walter Crane.

[2] This hall was enlarged in 1884. In 1902 it was fitted up as a
Library, and is now (1932) to be converted into a lecture hall with
a raised stage.

[3] It may be noted that the first building at Newnham College, the
Old Hall, was designed with a view to its being used as a private
house if the College should prove a failure. This was a condition
imposed by the ground landlords (St John's College), lest they should
be left with a useless building on their hands.

1873, the rooms were only just far enough advanced to be got ready for occupation by the students, fifteen in number; Miss Lumsden also came into residence as Classical Tutor. Madame Bodichon, who was, as Miss Davies said, "a perfect treasure on the Building Committee", threw herself into the details of furniture and fittings, and together they spent laborious days at Girton, arranging curtains and blinds, getting windows to open properly, and generally seeing to the thousand and one things wanted in a new house. Dame Frances Dove's description of her arrival at Girton gives a vivid impression of it:

As my home was in Lincolnshire, it so happened that I was the first to arrive.... The whole space between the building and the Huntingdon Road where the grass tennis courts now are was full of builders' debris, heaps of bricks, empty cement-tubs, baulks of wood, heaps of mortar and sand, shavings, etc. There were no windows or doors on the ground floor, the staircase was covered with planks, and as I entered, Miss Davies in her white shawl came flying down the stairs most kindly to receive me. She had rather an anxious look on her face, and she escorted me up to my room.... There were no door-posts up, no blinds or curtains, but there was a beautiful fire and I did not feel dismayed. Poor Miss Davies's troubles were yet to come. In an hour or two the whole of the new year arrived.... Miss Lumsden, I think, had come back as Classical tutor, and it fell to her lot...to smooth over the series of difficulties which faced the new-comers, for the corridor outside our rooms was full of carpenters' benches, their tools lying about in all directions, and you had to be very careful not to sweep quantities of shavings into your room as you entered.[1] As we had only wax candles to carry about, it certainly was a mercy that the whole College was not burnt down.... However, we soon settled in. Miss Davies's pluck was contagious, and after a few weeks she gave a big party. Mr Llewelyn Davies came down from London to help her. The biggest lecture room was made to look nice, and we all ran about putting down our nicest rugs, carrying the best armchairs we could find, and hanging pictures, and this first festival was thoroughly enjoyed. The mornings, of course, we all devoted to work, though I found it somewhat difficult to wrestle with the intricacies of trigonometry with the carpenters hammering up the door-posts outside my room....

I remember being charmed and delighted on answering a tap at my door to find that my visitor was Lady Stanley of Alderley.... Lady Stanley sat down and enquired kindly about our work and our comforts, and left me a most delightful remembrance of herself in the form of a student's box containing compasses, etc., with an inscription in her own handwriting on the outside. I still treasure that box.

Miss Davies wrote to Madame Bodichon that they had pulled through the first term bravely in spite of difficulties. "Many windows were wanting, and it was long before we had outer doors. To the last there was neither bell nor lock to our principal door." But, she continued, "altogether the building gives great satisfaction and I think the students were agreeably disappointed in the pleasantness of the situation". Miss Davies's delight in the growth of the College led her to see it in the gayest colours. To the Hitchin students their new abode seemed less attractive. The

[1] Your skirt of course touched the ground.

bare unfinished building, standing in flat windswept fields, without trees, lawns, or flower beds, seemed a poor exchange for the old house on the hill at Hitchin with its lovely views, and the pleasant garden sheltered by trees. Everything looked raw and unfinished; there were no gates, and the grounds were open to invasions of undergraduates, who came in parties of half a dozen walking together arm in arm.[1] Rumour said that some of them penetrated into the College and walked along the corridors, and that two professors were seen climbing the builders' ladders and inspecting the Mistress's rooms through her windows. Her rooms were not luxurious; the sitting-room chimney smoked, and the furniture was far from complete. The College was too poor to be comfortable, and every penny had to be saved towards paying for the building.

It was, however, immediately apparent that great benefits were resulting from the removal to Girton, and the greater proximity to Cambridge. Much interest had been roused at Cambridge in the higher education of women, and the influence of Professor Sidgwick led many members of the University, including some of the most conservative, to be favourable to the women students. In 1873, twenty-two out of the thirty-four professors then existing opened their courses to women. More followed later, and intercollegiate lectures also gradually became avail-

[1] While the College was building, undergraduates used to come to see it, and would give the bricklayers 6d. in return for the privilege of laying a brick.

able. Though there was as yet but little in the way of laboratory accommodation in the University, women students were generously received by Professor Liveing, Professor Humphry, and Professor Michael Foster. Attendance at the science lectures had its trials, and at first the students felt it "dreadfully uncomfortable". At Professor Humphry's lectures they sat modestly at the back in a little row by themselves, sometimes with Miss Davies as chaperone; and when a specimen of the human brain was passed round for inspection, they became aware that the undergraduates in front had all turned round to see whether this would discompose the ladies. Their quiet demeanour, however, had its effect, and at the end of the first term the lecturer complimented the men on their good behaviour under this trial. Professor Michael Foster's lectures in Biology were attended by Girton students, who sat in a gallery where they had their microscopes at a low window, and the demonstrator went up to help them in their seclusion.

To the undergraduates, the handful of women students were an eccentric novelty, and there was but little contact between them, apart from lectures and demonstrations. Societies such as the Students' Christian Union, the Heretics, the Moral Sciences Club, where men and women students began to find a common meeting ground, were growths of a much later date. As to outdoor games, there was at first very little provision at Girton. Games were not universal even among men as they are now, and had hardly begun to be played by women. There were no lawns round the College, nothing at first but ploughed fields on every side. To Miss Davies a garden was a luxury which must give way to more pressing needs. Beauty and amenities held a subordinate place in her view of life. Her whole soul was set upon the cause for which she was fighting, and every effort, every penny, was dedicated to it—nothing must be uselessly frittered away. This austerity was enhanced by a kind of aloofness—"I don't think I am as genuinely sociable as the Mistress here ought to be", she wrote to Mr Tomkinson. "I always said I could not be as much to them in this way as Mistress as I could as Secretary. One cannot play with them on quite equal terms as I used to do, and maintain authority as its sole representative." She felt this as a drawback, and did not like being Mistress. In her heart she was not in the least aloof, but was keenly interested in the students, and had a specially active sympathy with girls of narrow means, to whom she showed much kindness and consideration, doing all she could to further their entering the College. She was always alert to what was going on among the students, and on the watch to keep the College on the right path; the students (as she was aware) called her "the little instigator". Her view was that they should be treated not as irresponsible girls (as was the tendency towards young unmarried women in those days) but as responsible women. They were to be free to take their own line and develop in their own way. In practice, however, she wanted that way to be guided by her own ideas of law and order, and she had what seemed to some of the students an excessive regard for the proprieties, which caused resentment against what they thought unnecessary restrictions.

Another difficulty arose from the fact that in her acute anxiety about the financial position of the College, Miss Davies was not very willing that resident lecturers should be appointed, whose salaries would be an expense, while they would occupy rooms which might be used for students. The students hoped that Miss Lumsden would remain as Resident Lecturer in Classics; and they also wanted her to be elected as a member of the Executive Committee, for they felt that, having been herself a student, she knew and understood their needs. Here they had the sympathy of some members of the Committee. "Miss Lumsden can be of immense use to the College", wrote Miss Metcalfe to Madame Bodichon. "You and Lady Stanley and Lady Rich all agreed that her social influence among the students was invaluable." Miss Metcalfe and Madame Bodichon accordingly decided to propose Miss Lumsden for election as a member of the governing body, while they expected her to remain at the College as resident tutor. Miss Davies was strongly against this, holding that no one bearing any office in the internal administration of the College ought to be a member of the governing body. "Miss Lumsden will not come back unless she is on the Committee", wrote Miss Metcalfe to Madame Bodichon. "It may be an anomalous position for us, but I think the College wants her.... *You* know how

fully the students appreciate her work amongst them.
... Miss Davies and Mr Tomkinson say there is no
work for a classical tutor, why then are the students
in despair that they are not to have her help, and feel
that their success is imperilled by not having resident
teaching?" Feeling was so strong among the students
that one of them went so far as to appeal to Madame
Bodichon in the matter. Her answer has not been
preserved, but we know what Miss Davies thought.
"I think Madame Bodichon goes too much by the
temporary opinions and tastes and requirements of
the existing generation of students", she wrote to
Miss Manning; and to Madame Bodichon: "I think
you are in much too great a hurry to get an old student
put on [the governing body]. It would be far better
to wait.... I have the strongest objection to this movement for putting the Mistress under the control of
the Students—for that is what it comes to". In the
confusion of issues which arose, there was something
to be said on both sides. Madame Bodichon evidently
felt it due to Miss Davies that her view should prevail,
for we soon after find Miss Davies writing to her:
"As to your saying the College is mine, you know
that is nonsense. It has taken all of us to get so far,
and it wants us all still". The proposal for Miss
Lumsden's election was withdrawn; Miss Lumsden
resigned her tutorship; and Miss Davies also resigned
her post as Mistress and returned to her home in
London.

The whole episode illustrates once more the difficulties besetting the attempt to found a College of

University standing, when there was hardly any woman with collegiate experience available for the governing body or as a resident authority. The students, too, had no tradition behind them. Young and inexperienced as most of them were, they were pioneers, and were accordingly inclined to estimate rather highly the amount of influence which their views should have with the governing body. If there had been some residents of an intermediate class at the College—lecturers or advanced students—these might have done something to ease the situation. But the difficulties gradually quieted down, the sympathetic and steadying force that was needed coming at this juncture from Miss Maynard and Miss Welsh, students who entered the College in 1873, and from Miss Kingsland (now Mrs Higgs) who was Resident Lecturer in Natural Sciences from 1875 to 1876. Madame Bodichon, while sympathizing with the needs of the students, understood the greatness of purpose underlying Miss Davies's actions, and did what she could to interpret. "I think we all felt the want in Miss Davies of genial wisdom and influence," she wrote to Miss Marks (afterwards Mrs Ayrton), "but where do young people, men or women, find that? We do our best to get it for our students, but I fear natural selection from books, people, and all sorts of influences alone can teach each of us wisdom. ...I do wish we had some direct moral teaching at Girton, and I do wish we could get an ideal of life infused into the students; but there is much to be done with the eighteen years of life before College, and until your ideal school is started, I do not see how we can do it. The College cannot do much more than give *quiet liberty* and *opportunity*, and Miss Davies never had any other idea. That is a great deal, and she who has an immense love of justice for women would die to give young women what she never had herself in early life, ah, die to get it for them, though she might hate every individual. She is intense for an idea, truly disinterested and great. I do not think anyone does her justice."

Lady Lubbock (Miss C. A. Herschel) has given us an interesting impression of the situation as it was when she came up in 1874:

When I came up in October 1874, the lack of cordiality between the authorities and some of the senior students was very perceptible. The episode which Mrs Townshend has described[1] was only one symptom of a general feeling of resentment against what the students considered an unwarrantable interference with their liberty. This disloyal spirit came very near to wrecking the whole experiment; but the danger of its spreading among the new students was, I think, averted by Miss Maynard's influence and Miss Welsh's tact. Miss Maynard was in her third year when I came to Girton; she admired and respected Miss Davies for her indomitable courage and perseverance, at the same time she had a warm personal friendship for the three famous pioneers, "Woodhead, Cook, and Lumsden". Her own interest being evangelical, she exercised a sobering influence in the college; and in her weekly Bible readings the younger students found a safe

[1] The acting at Hitchin. See *ante*, p. 46.

anchorage when their faith was shaken by the rather aggressive agnosticism of some of the champions of freedom.[1]

New interests which arose were of course a help. There was much religious activity in Cambridge at this time, and mission services were held by undergraduates in the villages near Cambridge, in which some of the Girton students would have liked to take part. This Miss Davies discouraged, but she was pleased when they visited in the parish and taught in the Sunday School (as she had herself done in her girlhood), "which I think it very good of them to do," she wrote to Madame Bodichon, "instead of wandering about for long walks, or reclining on the grass these fine summer days". There were also fresh interests in the shape of games—lawn tennis and racquets were the first; and societies sprang up in numbers, as will be more fully described in Chapter ix. The inner life of the College was always vigorous, and as it grew in numbers, the energies of the students found their outlet more and more in developing new activities among themselves. Mrs Adam, writing of Girton in the 'eighties, describes the intense enjoyment, the overcrowded interests, "for we were run off our legs about as much as the youngest twentieth-century student, though less of our energy went into evening discussion meetings in Cambridge". In essentials, as she observes, "the life of students at Girton seems to remain true to itself".

Miss Lumsden on leaving Girton became a pioneer in another branch of education, creating a new type

[1] *Girton Review*, May Term, 1926.

of girls' school with the foundation of St Leonards School, St Andrews, a school which has always had many ties with Girton. Miss Davies went back to her work in London as Honorary Secretary to the College. There was no permanent Chairman, and she performed most of the duties of such an official, keeping a firm hand on all the College business. In 1877 a Secretary was appointed (Mrs Croom Robertson) who worked in close touch with Miss Davies and relieved her of the burden of routine work; and Miss Davies became Treasurer for a time, in succession to Mr Tomkinson. Mrs Croom Robertson was succeeded in 1882 by Miss Frances Kensington, who for fifteen years gave faithful and unselfish service. She combined a high standard of work with a kindness and courtesy, of which her beautiful handwriting was as it were a reflection—it never degenerated by constant use, though the typewriter was then an unknown instrument. Miss Davies resumed her post as Honorary Secretary in 1882, retaining it for twenty-two years. The Bursarship was held during this time successively by Mrs Croom Robertson, Miss Davies, Miss Kensington, and Miss M. Pickton, a niece of Sir Joshua Fitch.

As these officials and many of the Executive Committee lived in London, the Committee meetings were at first all held there; later, they were held at Girton in term time and in London during the vacation. The arrangement had the drawback, which gradually became increasingly felt, of making a marked separation between the business side of the College and its internal administration; but this was inevitable in the circumstances.

CHAPTER V

GROWTH AND CONSOLIDATION 1875–1903

The Mistress-ship. Miss Bernard (1875–85). The Graces of 1881. Differences of policy between Girton and Newnham. Growth of buildings at Girton. Miss Welsh's Mistress-ship (1885–1903). Miss Jones appointed Mistress.

THE College had now been in existence for six years, and during that time had had no less than four Mistresses. The position of the Mistress and her relations to the students and to the Executive Committee had not been clearly established, and the problems involved had become obscured by Miss Davies's tenure of the two offices of Secretary and Mistress. It was urgently necessary that the whole subject should be thoroughly considered and placed on a stable footing. The Committee, after reviewing the situation, defined the position of the Mistress in such a way as to make her of paramount importance as regards the internal management of the College, while herself remaining outside the governing body. She was to be responsible for all educational arrangements, as well as for discipline and domestic administration. The resident lecturers were to be appointed by the Committee on her nomination. The post was one involving a variety of work and much attention to detail. The duties shared to-day among the Directors of Studies, the Junior

Bursar, the Librarian, and other officials were then all performed by the Mistress.

These matters having been settled, the post was advertised, and on June 28th, 1875, Miss M. F. Bernard was appointed. Miss Bernard was niece to Lord Lawrence, with whom she had spent some time in India during his Viceroyalty. A course of training at the Home and Colonial Training College in Gray's Inn Road (founded in 1836 for elementary teachers) was all the special preparation she had had. Hers was a pioneer's work; as the first Mistress under the new *régime*, she had to put the Committee's plans into practice, to work out a system of discipline (no easy matter), and to create a tradition. To this task she brought a high sense of duty, and a power of keeping steadily on her course while co-operating readily with others. With much personal distinction and charm, she had a cool judgment and a manner of austere dignity, which was something of a bar to intimacy with the students, though beneath it there lay a real interest in their welfare. Her position was a solitary one, owing to the absence of colleagues. At first there was only one Resident Lecturer (in Natural Sciences), Miss Kingsland (now Mrs Higgs), who left in 1876, when Miss Welsh was appointed Resident Lecturer in Classics. In 1878 another Lecturer (in Natural Sciences) was added, in the person of Miss C. A. Herschel (now Lady Lubbock); not till 1880, when Miss C. A. Scott was appointed Resident Lecturer in Mathematics, were there so many as three. Not till many years afterwards was the College able to have research students. It was very small, isolated, and self-contained, but (as we have seen) it had in it great vitality, and the students of those days were able to lead busy, happy, active, ambitious lives, under circumstances which to modern eyes seem narrow and hampering. One notable point of contact with Cambridge occurred in 1885, when a Girton student, Miss Janet Case, took the part of Athena in the *Eumenides*, which was performed by the University in that year. This arose out of the performances of the *Electra* of Sophocles given by the students at Girton in 1883—performances of outstanding merit, which attracted a good deal of attention. But the invitation to Miss Case to join in the Greek play led to no further co-operation in University activities.

With Miss Bernard's Mistress-ship, a period of quiet work began, during which the women's Colleges made steady unostentatious progress, greatly helped by the development of girls' schools. The Girls' Public Day School Company was founded in 1872, and during the first fifteen years of Girton's existence, no less than twenty-eight day schools were opened in various parts of the country by that Company alone, and many schools were started by other agencies. There began to be a flow of students from the schools to the Colleges, and many of these students returned to the schools as teachers, eager in their turn to send pupils to the Colleges. The whole movement gained in strength and solidity, raising the standard of teaching throughout the country, for private teachers as well as in schools, though its influence was hardly as yet perceived by the world at large. The elements of a College had been brought into existence and were being developed surely, if slowly.

But there was one thing wanting, without which the very existence of the College remained precarious—official recognition by the University. Provision had been made when Girton was incorporated in 1872 for three members representing the University to have a share in its government; and in 1880 the Council of the Senate was prevailed upon to appoint three such members—Mr Austen Leigh of King's College, Professor Adams (the great astronomer), and Professor Liveing of St John's College— a constant friend to Girton. It was encouraging to have secured even this slight official link with the University, but it made no real change in the position, which remained quite insecure so long as admission to examinations and lectures depended on the personal goodwill of University men. Occasional refusals did occur, and there was always the risk of a complete breakdown. In 1877, an attempt was made to regularize the position through Parliament. An amendment proposed by Mr Leonard Courtney to the Universities of Oxford and Cambridge Bill, for enabling the Universities "to examine female students concurrently with male students", was rejected by 239 votes to 119.

This was discouraging, and the women's Colleges resigned themselves to patience, in the hope that their students would continue to be tolerated informally, and that the longer this went on, the more difficult would rejection become. But in 1880 the matter was taken out of their hands by a movement from outside. In that year a Girton student, Miss C. A. Scott, obtained a high place in the Mathematical Tripos; the exact places of women candidates were not published, but it became known that she was equal to the eighth wrangler. This success created a great impression in Cambridge. "She has completely won over one of the examiners, who wished to refuse to examine, by her success", wrote Miss Marks to Madame Bodichon. "He wanted to petition the Senate to grant the Degrees." Much interest was also felt in the world outside; and Mr and Mrs W. S. Aldis, of Newcastle, on their own initiative, got up a memorial to the Cambridge Senate asking for the admission of women not only to examinations but to degrees. A surprising amount of interest was aroused all over the country, and the memorial quickly assumed much larger proportions than its originators had expected. The authorities of Girton and Newnham were naturally alarmed, since the University was well known to be jealous of outside interference, and they feared the loss of even the toleration that had so far been accorded. But the thing could not be stopped, and the Girton authorities therefore decided to send a statement to the Council of the Senate in which, while disclaiming all part in the memorial, they expressed the view that the experiment of admitting women to University examinations had been sufficiently tested during the past ten years to justify their admission to the B.A. degree. The authorities of

Newnham took a different line. Professor Sidgwick's first interest was in education, not in admission to degrees, and he thought it most unwise to run the risk of raising opposition by asking for degrees at this juncture. The Association for Promoting the Higher Education of Women, under his guidance, sent in a statement to the Senate saying nothing about degrees, but intimating that they would welcome any arrangement by which the examination of women could be placed on a formal footing. The statements sent in by the two Colleges did not conflict; they ignored each other's point of view.

A Syndicate was thereupon appointed by the Senate, which reported in December, 1880, in favour of allowing women to take the Previous and Tripos Examinations on the same conditions as those required from members of the University, except in one respect, that the women students might, if they wished, substitute certain parts of the Higher Local for the Previous Examination, and thus escape the necessity for learning Latin and Greek. The Poll Degree examinations were in future to be closed to women. A number of memorials were organized in favour of these proposals, and although strong opposition was expected, when the Graces embodying them came before the Senate on February 24th, 1881, they were passed by the very unexpected majority of 398 votes to 32.

The effect was, that the women's Colleges were recognized by the University, to this extent, that their students were admitted to honours examinations.

Officially the University was to them what the University of London was for many years to all its students—an examining body and nothing more. Admission to University lectures and laboratories continued to be unofficial, and subject to the permission of the individual lecturer. As regards admission to the University Library, neither students nor lecturers at the women's Colleges could use it except to the very limited extent allowed to the general public. But an increasing number of University and intercollegiate lectures were opened to women students, who were also taught by Cambridge men at Girton and Newnham (as well as by their own resident lecturers). This teaching was of course invaluable, and the women's Colleges had many staunch friends in the University, without whose help they could never have been carried on at all. The students thus came into direct touch with Cambridge teachers: but the resident lecturers meanwhile had no link with the University beyond friendly personal relations with the Cambridge men who taught at Girton and Newnham.

But the drawbacks hardly seemed to count at the moment, in the delightful sense of security gained. There was no more fear lest examiners should decline to act; the names of the successful candidates were in future to be officially published; and the University was to grant a certificate to each successful woman candidate. "What we gain", wrote Miss Davies to Madame Bodichon, "is that what we have been doing all along by favour, will now be secured as a right."

The position thus gained was to remain unaltered for close on forty years; and during the earlier part of this period, the difference in policy already noticed between Girton and Newnham continued in force, with this effect, that the special permission accorded by the University, for women students to take certain parts of the Higher Local Examination in place of the Latin and Greek papers in the Previous Examination, was used by Newnham students but not by Girtonians. Girton students therefore took precisely the same course of examinations for degrees in honours as men students; Newnham students in very many cases did not. Newnham students were also allowed by the College authorities to take the Higher Local Examination as an end in itself, instead of a Tripos. This provided a shorter course than the regular three years, and by this means the demand for the teachers, so urgently needed in the schools now springing up everywhere, was met more quickly than would otherwise have been possible. As the schools became more efficient, and women students came up better prepared, the Higher Local was gradually dropped by Newnham, and the students practically all took Triposes. Girton and Newnham became more and more alike in their methods, and their aims have now for many years been identical.

Even before the position of Girton had been stabilized by the Graces of 1881, the process of enlarging the College had already begun. Soon after Miss Bernard's appointment as Mistress, in 1875, a scheme was adopted for building eighteen sets of

students' rooms and three lecture rooms at a cost of
£5000. A Building Committee, consisting of Miss
Davies, Madame Bodichon, and Lady Stanley of
Alderley, set to work, and the wearisome task of
raising funds had to be resumed. The debt on the
original buildings had not been fully paid, though the
College was being forced into expansion. For many
years this state of things was continually repeated,
each access of numbers involving fresh struggles and
expedients for raising money. These financial cam-
paigns were organized and carried through by Miss
Davies with unremitting pertinacity and diligence.
Some of the City Companies—in particular the
Clothworkers, Drapers, Skinners and Goldsmiths—
gave valuable support in providing scholarships and
in subscribing to the general funds of the College.
But for the most part, subscribers were seldom to be
found among people who could afford to give large
sums. In 1876 eighteen students' rooms and three
lecture rooms were added to the little original block
of buildings, prolonging them to the west, and
forming the northern end of the Hospital wing; this
cost £5000, and at the same time Lady Stanley gave
£600 with which to build the first laboratory. The
small block projecting to the west between the
Hospital and Orchard wings was also added at this
time; it was for many years called "the Taylor knob",
because it was built with the help of a gift of £1000
from Mr and Mrs Thomas Taylor, whose daughter,
Miss E. H. Taylor, had intended to enter the College,
but was prevented by her early death. In 1879, the

rest of the Hospital wing was added, at a cost of £7000; then for a few years there was comparative freedom from building, except for the lodge at the front gate, which was given by Lady Stanley in 1880.

The demand for admission was, however, still growing, and in 1884 the Orchard wing was added, together with the porch, and the rooms over it, at the end of the Hospital wing. The Stanley Library and the Mistress's rooms over it were built at this time; the dining hall and the accommodation for servants were enlarged, and the pond was made. The College could now hold eighty students. The cost, over £12,000, was partly met by a gift from Madame Bodichon of £5000, subject to a charge of £250 per annum to be paid to her during her life. Lady Stanley gave £1000 towards the cost of the new library (named after her on her death in 1895)—"the Library which we have so long and so urgently needed", as a student wrote in the *Girton Review*. "We are already wondering how we contrived to do without it in the Dark Ages before it was built." Miss Florence Ward (a former student of the College, now Mrs C. G. Montefiore) was appointed as the first Librarian.

In 1885 Miss Bernard resigned the post of Mistress on her marriage to Dr P. W. Latham of Cambridge. It was now at last possible to appoint an old student of the College as her successor—Miss Welsh. Miss Welsh had already resided at the College for nine years as classical lecturer and Vice-Mistress, and some thought it rather an uninspiring appointment. But it proved an excellent one; her kindly wit and wisdom, her sound judgment and remarkable insight into character, enabled her to establish right relations both with the students and with Miss Davies; and hers was the chief influence in establishing a tradition of loyalty and affection between the students and the Mistress. Her qualities seemed to grow with the demands made upon them as the College increased in numbers. Her relations with the past students were particularly happy, and very valuable to the College. In addition to the Mistress-ship, she held the post of Garden Steward, to which she had already been appointed in 1883; the garden, though it gave her a great deal to do, afforded a welcome change from the exacting routine of her work within the College.

Not long after Miss Welsh had taken up her appointment as Mistress, a fresh addition to the College buildings was made possible through the generosity of a previously unknown benefactress, Miss Jane Catherine Gamble,[1] who left her residuary estate, amounting to about £19,000, to Girton. This was a gift far exceeding anything that had hitherto been received. Seventeen acres of land were bought on the Cambridge side of the College, bringing the property up to the junction of the Girton and Huntingdon roads. The acquisition of this land was an immense advantage to the College. Part of it became under Miss Welsh's care the delightful grounds known as "Woodlands". The buildings were increased by the addition in 1887 of the Tower wing, and the number of students was brought up

[1] See Biographical Index.

THE EMILY DAVIES COURT, SHOWING THE STANLEY LIBRARY, 1884

to 104. This naturally threw a heavier burden upon the Mistress, who was tutor to all the students, and every day saw many of them individually about questions of work and discipline. Some relief was given to her by the creation of a new post, that of Junior Bursar, to whom was given the management of the household, the land, and the buildings. The Librarian, Miss Florence Ward, was appointed as Junior Bursar, being succeeded by Miss Constance Jones as Librarian. After two years, her place as Junior Bursar was taken in 1891 by Miss Gertrude Jackson, a former mathematical student of the College. It is hard to imagine how the administration could have been carried on without such an officer.

Large as Miss Gamble's legacy was, even more was quickly spent, and the College was again in debt; but a further extension was again soon needed. Miss Davies had a plan all ready for building on a magnificent scale. Lady Stanley was opposed to the scheme, on financial grounds, and it was dropped for the time, but under Miss Davies's vigilant guidance, every penny that could be saved was set aside for building. On Madame Bodichon's death, after many years of ill health, in 1891, the College received from her a legacy of £10,000; and after Lady Stanley's death in 1895, the building scheme was revived. By this time, the College had actually succeeded by the strictest economy in saving nearly £8000 out of income, and another £8000 was promised by subscribers. The total wanted was £50,000, which was still far off, but Miss Davies determined to push the scheme through. Her zeal and determination carried the day, and the largest addition of all was made, including the present dining hall and kitchens, the chapel, the Woodlands wing, and the block connecting it with the chapel. The number of students was now raised to about 140, and something had to be done to lighten the Mistress's task: Directors of Studies were appointed from among the resident lecturers, to relieve her of the organization of the students' work.

The buildings were completed by 1902, and as usual they brought with them a load of debt—this time on a hitherto unknown scale, the estimates having been very much exceeded. A temporary advance of £20,000 from the College bankers was succeeded by a mortgage to the Prudential Assurance Company for no less than £40,000. The interest on loans amounted to about £1500 per annum, and during the next twelve years the history of the College is a dreary tale of financial struggle. Probably under Mr Tomkinson's guidance these troubles would have been avoided, but he had for many years been unable owing to ill health to take any part in the affairs of the College.

In 1903, Miss Welsh resigned the office of Mistress, after twenty-seven years of devoted service to the College. She was succeeded by Miss Constance Jones, also a former student of the College, who was Resident Lecturer in Moral Sciences (1884–1916), Librarian (1890–3), and Vice-Mistress (1896–1903). Miss Jones was first and foremost a scholar and student, and it was fortunate that the new arrangements made it possible for her to continue working at her own subjects to some extent. With gentle, unassuming manners, she was very sociable; and though by nature and inclination she was not an administrator, her high sense of duty and power of adaptability enabled her to carry on the work of the Mistress. Her intellectual interests were wide, ranging, as Miss Welsh said, from theology and literature to music and architecture. The period of her Mistress-ship was one of great financial difficulty, marked nevertheless by distinct progress. Almost immediately after she had assumed office, she was confronted with as great a crisis as had occurred in the history of the College—the resignation of Miss Davies. But the events which led to this must be left for another chapter.

Before proceeding any further with the internal history of Girton something must be said of its relations to the University. While the College was growing steadily in size and efficiency and scope, its relations with the University remained officially at a standstill. The success of 1881, when the Senate passed the Graces which admitted students of the women's colleges to honours examinations, raised high hopes of admission to the University which were not fulfilled. An attempt to gain admission was made in 1887, when a Girton student, Miss A. F. Ramsay (afterwards Mrs Montagu Butler) was placed in the first division of the first class of the Classical Tripos, while of the men who took the same examination, none were placed higher than the second division. Miss Ramsay, if she had been a man, would therefore have been Senior Classic, and the event attracted a great deal of public attention. Queen Victoria presented a signed photograph of herself to Miss Ramsay; and *Punch* brought out a cartoon of himself respectfully showing her into a railway carriage marked "First Class, For Ladies Only". Miss Davies seized the opportunity to organize a movement for asking the Senate for the admission of women to degrees. A Committee was formed consisting of Miss Davies herself, her brother Mr Llewelyn Davies, Lady Stanley of Alderley, Lady Goldsmid, and Mrs Garrett Anderson; with some Cambridge residents, notably Professor Liveing and Dr Henry Jackson, both of whom had always been staunch friends to Girton and were for many years on the Executive Committee. Dr Jackson was in favour of the admission of women to the University on the same terms as men, and he threw himself into the cause with all the weight of his vigorous personality and great influence. But the movement failed, the Council of the Senate refusing even to appoint a Syndicate to consider the question. Ten years later, another attempt of the same kind was set on foot. This time, the initial move came from Newnham, in consequence of a widespread and growing opinion that women who had passed the Cambridge examinations were handicapped in their subsequent careers by want of degrees. A Syndicate appointed to consider the question produced a report recommending the admission of women to titular degrees, but making no other change in the position. Even this was rejected, on May 21st, 1897, by 1707 votes to 661.

A suggestion that a separate University should be created for women, first made in 1887, was again brought forward in 1897, and was fully discussed at a conference organized by the Governors of the Royal Holloway College, who were then considering whether they should seek power to confer degrees on their students. In the course of the discussion it became perfectly clear that, as Mr James Bryce said, "No one who is concerned with the education of women as a teacher, whether a man or a woman, is in favour of having a separate university for women". By that date, all the Universities except Oxford and Cambridge admitted women as members on equal terms with men, and it had become clear that the immense task of creating a new University needed all the support to be gained from both sexes, and that any principle of exclusion or limitation would only be a source of weakness.

In 1904 the difficulties experienced by Cambridge women through not being admitted to degrees were to some extent met by the action of Trinity College, Dublin, where degrees were for about three years thrown open to qualified women from other Universities. About 200 Girtonians availed themselves immediately of this permission, and more followed. The past students of Girton and Newnham who took these degrees were mostly women engaged in the teaching profession, to whom a degree was especially important, and who felt the want of it the more because the degrees of London and the newer Universities had long been open to women.

CHAPTER VI

A TIME OF TRANSITION 1903-1922

Research work in the University. Movement for its endowment at
Girton. Movement for changes in the government of Girton.
Resignation of Miss Davies. Permanent Chairman of the Council.
The Girton College Roll. The War. Miss Jex-Blake's Mistress-ship
(1916-22). Jubilee of the College. Gifts for endowment of research.
Royal Commission on the Universities. Titular degrees. Decision to
apply for a Charter.

WITH the extension of 1902, the College
attained to something approaching its full
stature. Miss Davies aimed at 200 students;
160 were now secured, and the kitchens and dining
hall were on such a scale as to make it possible to add
rooms for more students when funds would allow.
But the process of growth had been a difficult one,
and the economies which had been necessary were a
serious hindrance to developments other than building. Equipment was kept at the lowest possible level;
the library and laboratories were greatly in need of
expansion; and there were no endowments for Fellowships or for research work. Miss Davies, in her
eagerness to open the doors of Girton to as large a
number of students as possible, had always set her
face against giving up rooms to research students,
and was not very willing even to encourage students
to stay on for a fourth year.

Research meanwhile was coming to occupy a more
and more important position in the University. While

the College was struggling into existence, profound changes were, as we have seen, being brought about at Cambridge. The Royal Commission of 1852 initiated a process of reorganization which had great results; men were attracted in quickly increasing numbers, and the Universities became a powerful educational force throughout the country. The curriculum, formerly so limited and narrow, was immensely enlarged; new Triposes were created for history, law, and modern languages; and other subjects were much expanded, more particularly in the domain of science. The problems of teaching came to be attacked from a new point of view, and new ideals of education were developed. In science there were opened new and unbroken fields of work, and the application of scientific methods stimulated investigation on new lines in the older fields of classics, philosophy, and history. Educational problems came to be considered from the point of view of the subject, as well as from that of the Colleges; the growth and furtherance of the subject was constantly in the minds of teachers and pupils; and research came to be an essential part of University life.

The influence of this new spirit was at first hardly felt by Girton. The earlier generations of women students, hampered by want of preparation for their work, could aim at nothing higher than success in a Tripos, and most of them on going down entered at once on the much needed work of teaching other women and girls. They had no opportunity for embarking on research; the College was too poor to set

aside endowments for this purpose; and the want of
relations with the University was a serious hindrance.
Nevertheless, women students were taught largely by
members of the University, through whom the new
influences gradually made themselves felt. As the
standard of women's education generally was raised
by the women's Colleges, the latter began to react to
the new spirit in the University, and the opinion
gained ground among the resident lecturers and past
students of Girton that want of provision for research
was keeping the College back, and preventing it from
becoming a place of real higher education, worthy of
admission to the University. Evidence of this is to
be found in the *Girton Review* so long ago as 1883.
In 1888 the Executive Committee of the College did
something to encourage post-graduate work by the
founding of the Gamble Prize, in commemoration
of Miss J. C. Gamble and her benefaction. A more
ambitious attempt was initiated by the past students
in 1892. After a subscription dinner of old students
held in that year a surplus of £5 remained in hand,
and at the suggestion of Miss Gertrude Jackson,
this small sum was set aside as the nucleus of a fund
for the endowment of a Studentship, for which Miss
Jackson and Miss Jex-Blake were trustees. The same
thing was done after subsequent dinners; subscriptions were also collected, and the fund was built up by
slow degrees.[1] In 1896, a petition from old students

[1] The income of the Old Girtonians' Studentship was usually given
as an augmentation to the Pfeiffer Studentship, till in 1912 it became
sufficient to support a research student on its own account.

to the Executive Committee (drafted by Miss Freund, Mrs Adam, and Miss E. M. Allen) resulted in the offer of a Studentship of £40 per annum from the Pfeiffer Fund.[1] In 1899 an old student, Miss Florence Durham, collected about £200 which provided a research studentship for three years.[2] These efforts represented a strong wish on the part of old students, but as regards practical results, they were almost negligible, and it remained hardly possible for any research to be carried on by Girtonians, except by the very few, among those qualified for the work, who had private means. Mrs Ayrton[3] was able to do some important work on electricity, and Miss Ethel Sargant[3] made a substantial contribution to botanical science from her laboratory at Reigate. Miss Sargant, who was a woman of much wisdom and practical good sense, appealed for the endowment of research at the women's Colleges in an article entitled "The Inheritance of a University", which appeared in the *Girton Review* for the Lent Term, 1901. She advocated the cause with her characteristic ability and breadth of view, but it led to no immediate results.

Past students were accordingly inclined to think that Girton was not moving sufficiently with the times, and not only as regards research but also as

[1] The first Pfeiffer Research Student was Mrs Walter Maunder, who used it for the undertaking of a photographic survey of the Milky Way.

[2] Awarded to Miss F. E. Cave-Browne-Cave, for the investigation of the distribution of frequency of the barometric height at various stations.

[3] See Biographical Index.

regards the governing body of the College. To many of them the governing body seemed unsatisfactory in two essential points—it was not sufficiently in touch either with the past students, or with the internal administration of the College. It will be remembered that when the College was incorporated in 1872, provision was made for three representative members of the governing body to be elected by the Certificated Students; who never met, the elections being conducted by means of voting papers sent by post. The desire to meet and discuss the affairs of the College led in 1879 to the establishment of an unofficial body, the Association of Certificated Students, which held annual meetings alternately at Girton and in London (those at Girton being usually in conjunction with the biennial subscription dinner of old students). In 1901 this body presented a memorial to the Executive Committee asking them "to consider the advisability of adding to the number of Past Students now serving as Members of the College". Under Miss Davies's guidance, Miss Dove, a student of the early days at Girton (now Dame Frances Dove), was co-opted as a Member of the College, but nothing was done to increase the number of elected representatives. As regards the question of internal administration, those responsible for the teaching and internal management of the College had no place, under the constitution, on the governing body; though the Mistress had been co-opted as a member since 1885, and one or two resident lecturers had been elected as their representatives by the Certificated Students. To these elections Miss Davies remained strongly opposed. Her ideal of government was the school type, with a Council from which the headmistress and her assistants should all be excluded.

On Miss Welsh's resignation in 1903, Miss Davies, aware of the growth of views opposed to her own, wrote a memorandum on the question, which she circulated among the Certificated Students. This drew forth a reply from a special meeting of their Association, which made it clear that it was the view of the majority of old students that the lecturers and other resident authorities should have a larger share in the government of the College. The Association had no power to do anything but express an opinion. But it was found that the majority of the Executive Committee agreed with them, and the new Mistress, Miss Jones, was elected a Member of the College and of the Executive Committee soon after her appointment. This defeat was a blow unexpected by Miss Davies, and after much consideration, in May, 1904, she resigned both the office of Honorary Secretary and her membership of the Executive Committee. She continued to be a Member of the College (the larger body, corresponding to the governors under the Charter), but she took no further part in affairs. Her interest in Girton remained as keen as ever; she continued her annual visits during the Long Vacation Term, and her relations with everyone there remained perfectly friendly. In defeat and withdrawal she showed her true dignity and greatness of character.

Miss Davies's retirement marked the end of an

epoch in the history of Girton. For thirty-six years she had devoted her life to its service, and her will had always been the predominating force in its counsels. There was, of course, no one who could fill her place, nor would this have been desirable. It was now necessary to learn how to do without her, and a difficult period of readjustment followed. A new Secretary, Miss Mary Clover, had been appointed only the year before Miss Davies's retirement. She was left to grapple with her duties as best she could; Miss Davies's guidance was removed, there was no permanent Chairman, and as the Secretary still lived and had her office in London, she was to a great extent cut off from the College. Fortunately Miss Kensington was at hand, as a member of the Executive Committee, and with all her former experience as Secretary was most helpful during this crisis. Miss Clover, who had been a student at the College from 1895 to 1898, had kept in touch with Girton, and had useful experience as Secretary of the Association of Certificated Students, and on the Committee of the Women's University Settlement, Southwark. Young as she was, her unselfish devotion and business capacity were invaluable during these critical years. No great change could be effected immediately; the financial situation overshadowed all else, and the Executive Committee was faced with the struggle to pay off the mortgage of £40,000 on the buildings without the help of its most active and experienced worker. In 1904, a gift was received of £2000 from Rosalind, Countess of Carlisle (daughter of Lady Stanley of

Alderley), but very little further progress was made till in 1909 a vigorous financial campaign was organized by some past students of the College, of whom the chief were Lady Dorothy Howard (Lady Carlisle's daughter, now Lady Henley), Mrs Walter Runciman, and Miss Honor Lawrence. By dint of much hard work the debt was by 1910 reduced to £29,000.

Preoccupied by these financial anxieties, it was difficult for the Mistress and the Committee to deal adequately with other matters, but nevertheless some changes were effected. It was now generally agreed that it was desirable that the Committee should be brought into closer touch with the teaching staff of the College, and that the latter should have more opportunities for taking a general view of their problems. An Education Board was therefore created in 1904, consisting of the Mistress, Vice-Mistress, and Directors of Studies, who were to discuss matters affecting educational work, and report to the Executive Committee. Presently, too, there came opportunities for moving the business offices of the College from London to Girton. In 1906, on the resignation of the Bursar, Miss Pickton, a Resident Bursar was appointed, Miss Eleanor Allen, who was already in residence as Librarian; and two years later the Secretary, Miss Clover, came to live in Cambridge, and though her office was still in her own house, she was able to keep in much closer touch with the College.[1] In 1910 a move was made towards bringing

[1] Since 1923 the Secretary's office has been in the College buildings.

the College staff into closer connection with the Council; the staff was asked to nominate a representative, who was then co-opted by the Council. Miss Meyer, Director of Studies in Mathematics, served in this way for a year, and was succeeded in 1911 by the Junior Bursar, Miss Reynard.

These were changes involving nothing in the way of expense; research was a much more difficult matter. A welcome gift had been received in 1902 of an endowment of £2000 for a Research Scholarship in memory of the distinguished economist John Elliott Cairnes, from his niece Miss Robertson. It is interesting to notice that two future Mistresses of the College received post-graduate benefits about this time. In 1902 Miss Wodehouse was awarded the Gilchrist Fellowship of £100, given by the Gilchrist Trustees, and tenable for one year alternately at Girton and at Newnham.[1] In 1903 the Pfeiffer Studentship was awarded to Miss Phillpotts (afterwards Dame Bertha Newall). The studentship was of the value of only £40 for one year, increased to £60 by the income of the Old Students' Studentship Fund which was added to it. With this small endowment she carried out a valuable piece of original work at Copenhagen, though the money was barely enough,

[1] The Gilchrist Fellowship was founded in 1900 by the Gilchrist Trustees to commemorate the interest taken by their Chairman, Mr R. Leigh Holland, in the higher education of women. The holder was required to follow a course of preparation for the profession of medicine or teaching or such other pursuit as might be approved by the Trustees. It was sometimes partly used for research. Since 1911 it has been entitled a Studentship.

and she had to come home all too soon, and penniless. The encouragement of post-graduate work was felt to be a matter of such urgency, that in spite of the debt a Research Studentship was granted out of College funds in 1904, and two fourth-year scholarships in the following year; two more being given, one by an old student, the other by the Mistress, Miss Constance Jones, who was in complete sympathy with the policy of encouraging advanced work.

Want of money barred the way to further progress; and it was difficult to proceed vigorously with a definite policy, so long as there was no regular Chairman. At last, in 1909, it was decided that the Chairman should be elected annually; and the office was filled by a succession of Cambridge men who might almost be described as a new generation of Founders—Dr William Cunningham, Fellow of Trinity and Archdeacon of Ely; Sir Hugh Anderson, Master of Caius College; Mr Arthur Berry, Fellow and Tutor of King's College; and Dr Giles, Master of Emmanuel College. Girton owes a great debt of gratitude to these four distinguished men, all deeply engaged in their work for the University and for their own Colleges, who gave such unwearied and unselfish service during this difficult time of transition.

Dr Cunningham, who had already been for many years a most generous and helpful friend to Girton, was elected Chairman[1] in 1909. A move was now made for the encouragement of post-graduate work.

---

[1] The title "Executive Committee" was dropped in 1911 for that of "Council".

It was decided in 1910 that a Studentship of £120 a year should be offered in place of the Scholarships hitherto granted out of the income of the Pfeiffer Fund. At the same time, the regulations of the Publication Fund were modified with a view to giving increased opportunities and stimulus to post-graduate work. This fund was the gift of Dr Cunningham who had had many pupils among the historical students at Girton, to whom he gave kindly help and encouragement. Miss McArthur (for many years resident lecturer), Miss Lamond, Professor Lilian Knowles, and others, owed much to his teaching. The Publication Fund consisted of the profits of his book, *The Growth of English Industry and Commerce*, given by him in 1898 for the purpose of publishing books by past students. He had a warm feeling for the College, and took an interest even in small details of administration. He was quite concerned when the time-honoured institution of "tray" in the evening was abolished, to be replaced by "jug", and declared in Council his unalterable affection for "tray"; but the Junior Bursar prevailed in this matter.

An object which Dr Cunningham had specially at heart was the establishment of a pension scheme on a contributory basis for the resident lecturers and administrative officers of the College. The need for such a scheme had long been apparent. The debt, as we have seen, stood at £29,000 in 1910; nevertheless the pension scheme was established in that year, on his initiative. In the following year, the outlook was brightened by a generous benefaction—the gift from

THE BUILDINGS AFTER 1887

Photo: Palmer Clarke

four anonymous donors of a Fellowship of £300 a year to be held at the College or elsewhere.[1] It was a great thing to have even one Fellowship of this magnitude.

Meanwhile, the Association of Certificated Students were pursuing their aim of establishing a stronger connection between themselves and the College. At a meeting of the Association held at Girton in February, 1908, it was resolved to appoint a Sub-Committee "to consider the ways and means for establishing closer relations between the Governing Body of Girton College and the past and present students". The members of the Sub-Committee were Miss Janet Case, Miss Florence Durham, Miss M. E. J. Taylor, Miss B. S. Phillpotts, and Miss Crewdson (Hon. Sec. of the G.C.A.C.S.), with Miss Honor Lawrence as their Secretary. They prepared a scheme, which with some modification was adopted by the College in 1911, and is known as the Girton College Roll. Without entering into full details, this may be described as a reorganization retaining the chief features of the two hitherto existing unofficial arrangements—the annual business meeting, and the biennial dinner at the College. The new body was placed in close official connection with the College by the appointment of a Registrar of the Roll, and by

[1] The first nomination, which was to be for life, was in the hands of the donors, who nominated Mrs Arthur Strong, Litt.D. Dublin, Hon. LL.D. St Andrews, a past student of Girton, author of various works on Archaeology, and for many years Assistant Director of the British School of Archaeology at Rome.

financial and other links, and it has ever since been an active force in the affairs of the College. Its first annual business meeting was held in London on January 13th, 1912; and on February 24th, 250 members were entertained at dinner at Girton. The Chairman of the Council, Dr Cunningham, was present, and afterwards welcomed the guests in a speech expressing his pleasure at the closer relation established between the College and its old students. He also spoke of the need for improved equipment, and expressed the opinion that the first thing to aim at was now the highest possible degree of efficiency rather than an increase in the number of students— a view with which his audience were in full sympathy.

Dr Cunningham resigned in 1913 and was succeeded by the Master of Caius, Dr (afterwards Sir Hugh) Anderson, who was a member of the Council from 1913 to 1916, and Chairman from 1913 to 1914. By 1912 the building debt had been reduced to £24,000, partly by the generosity of Miss Davies and Mrs Garrett Anderson, who each gave £1000. Substantial help was also given by City Companies, especially by the Drapers, Skinners, Salters, Grocers, and Clothworkers. Mrs Eva McLaren gave £500 in memory of her sister, Miss H. Müller, a former student of the College. A new benefactor now came to the rescue, Mr (afterwards Sir Alfred) Yarrow, who most generously offered to pay half of the debt, provided the other half could be collected by January 1st, 1914. No greater piece of good fortune could have befallen the College. Mr Yarrow's gift came just in time to save it from disaster. The friends of the College threw themselves into the task of collecting the money required. Success was achieved; the mortgage was paid off on January 8th, 1914, and the College released from debt just in time to enable it to weather the period of storm and stress which set in with the war. The financial skill and experience of the Master of Caius were most helpful during this critical year; and later, as a member of the Royal Commission on the Universities (1919) and of the Cambridge Statutory Commission, his inner knowledge of Girton and sympathy with the needs of the women's Colleges proved of the greatest value. His successor as Chairman was Mr Arthur Berry, Fellow of King's College, who had for many years lectured on mathematics at Girton, and since 1899 had been a member of the Executive Committee (later the Council). He had already given generously of his time and thoughts to the College. Not only his distinguished ability, but his transparent sincerity, disinterestedness, and kindness, made his presence at the Council specially valuable.

The College was now at last free from debt, and the Council were looking forward to a new era of progress. To begin with, three Fellowships were instituted, of £150 a year each, tenable for three years, and named after three benefactors, Lady Carlisle, Sir Alfred Yarrow, and Mrs Emily Pfeiffer. Some very necessary improvements to the buildings were also planned, including a new system of drainage, and the installation of electric light. The buildings had hitherto been lighted with gas in the corridors only, and with oil lamps and candles in the rooms. Estimates had already been passed, and the orders were about to be given, when the situation was suddenly and entirely changed, in August, 1914, by the outbreak of war. It was felt to be impossible to proceed. All hopes of progress were brought to a standstill. It was no time for running risks; the only thing to do was to carry on normal activities so far as they were possible, and how far that would be, no one could tell. The abnormal situation quickly made itself felt at Girton. Mr Berry was obliged to resign the Chairmanship in 1915, owing to his appointment to a post with the Mediterranean Expeditionary Force. It was hard to replace him at a time when the younger men were all wanted for war service, and the burden of University work had to be borne by the older men; but Dr Cunningham, with wonderful generosity and public spirit, resumed the office of Chairman.

In the following year, 1916, Miss Constance Jones resigned the Mistress-ship and was succeeded by Miss Jex-Blake, who had been principal Resident Lecturer in Classics since 1885, Director of Studies since 1902, and Vice-Mistress since 1903. An article in the *Girton Review* welcomed her in the following terms:

Not only the College, but the whole educational world owes Miss Jex-Blake a debt of gratitude for the part she has taken in encouraging advanced study and research.... Those who have experienced her rule as Mistress during the Long Vacation Term know how graciously and judiciously she has performed her temporary duties.... But it is to the classical students of Girton, past and present, that the news of Miss Jex-Blake's appointment will cause the most intense satisfaction. They, to whom she has been "guide, philosopher, and friend", have to thank her not only for wise direction and unfailing kindness, but also for the high standard of work always inculcated by her, which is in the widest sense a possession for ever.

What the classical students owed to Miss Jex-Blake has been well expressed in a speech by one of her pupils, Dr M. D. Brock: "To her as a teacher we owe far more than the actual knowledgem iparted to us—we owe, I think, an attitude of mind, a respect for truth, for clear thought and clear expression.... Her teaching was always human and alive....No one else ever taught like that". The results achieved speak for themselves in the College records; one illustration may be noted. Towards the end of her Mistress-ship, pupils of hers were holding classical lectureships not only at Girton, but at Lady Margaret Hall, Newnham, Somerville, Bedford (where there were two), and Holloway Colleges, not to mention many important posts in schools. The "wise direction" and the "high standard" maintained for so many years at Girton, were a power not only among the classical students; they were always an unfailing source of strength to the College, more especially during the war and the difficult years immediately after it.

In those anxious times, the task of keeping the College going was no easy one. A possible shortage of students, alarms as to Zeppelin raids, difficulties as to labour, food, fuel, and finance, all these had to be coped with. The Council were resolved to do their utmost to keep up the numbers and efficiency of the students, since the best contribution that the College could make towards the country's need was clearly a supply of trained and competent women. The calls for war service resulted in some empty rooms; the falling off was slight, but every diminution of income from students' fees added to the difficulties caused by the great increase in prices and wages which set in in 1916. The problem of feeding the students and keeping them warm was a serious one. Coal and food were not only dear but scarce; both were rationed; eggs (to take one instance) rose at one time to the fantastic price of 9d. apiece. Labour was scarce, when men were being called up to the army, and maids were going to earn war wages in munition factories. Yet the garden had to be kept going (here the students helped) in order to grow potatoes and other vegetables for food; the breeding of pigs was started and became an important item in the budget. Besides losing its Chairman, the College lost two lecturers (Miss Ivens and Miss Drew) who undertook war work of various kinds; those who remained did what they could in their spare time, the mathematical lecturers making calculations for the War Office, others serving on Committees, visiting hospitals, knitting, and so forth. The College Secretary, Miss Clover, filled the exacting post of General Service Superintendent at the First Eastern General Hospital (a temporary hospital on the site of the new University Library) from 1916 to 1919, while carrying on her usual work for the

College. Three Belgian students were received at the College for a year without fees, and one Serbian for five terms at a greatly reduced fee.

Meanwhile past students were taking their share (like other women) and proving their worth in all sorts of national work. The services of educated women were quickly appreciated as the authorities and the public came to realize what they could do. The demand for women to replace masters in boys' schools became far greater than the supply. By 1918 public schools such as Rugby had Girtonians on the staff. Eighteen Girtonians are known to have replaced teachers at Universities, in two cases filling the posts of professors absent on war service. Outstanding work was done by Mrs Ayrton, who invented a gas-dispelling fan; by Miss Phillpotts as private secretary to Sir Esmé Howard (now Lord Howard of Penrith), the British Minister at Stockholm; and by Miss Sargant, who left her home at the Old Rectory, Girton, and went to live in London in order to organize a Register of University Women prepared to undertake work of national importance. (This Register was afterwards incorporated in the Register of Professional Women maintained at the Ministry of Labour.) The Royal Society awarded a Lawrence Studentship of £160 to Miss Dufton in 1916 for investigating pneumonia caused by gas poisoning. A Hospital Unit equipped by subscriptions from Girton and Newnham, and partly manned by past students, served throughout the war in France and in the Balkans. An impetus to the medical education of women was naturally given by the war, and in 1916 the University decided to admit women to the First and Second M.B. Examinations—the first concession to women students since 1881. In medicine, nursing, the Civil Service, agriculture, munitions, and in the innumerable organizations to which the war gave birth, past students of the women's Colleges proved their value. One permanent result was that the number and variety of openings for women on leaving College, already much larger than in the early days, was greatly increased. A comment from the *Girton Review* may be quoted, made on the occasion of a Roll Dinner in 1923:

There were some two hundred and fifty old students assembled at Girton this week-end; and the wide range of their occupations is in itself perhaps the greatest tribute which could be paid to the sound training which this college gave them, and to the tradition of service, which Miss Lumsden emphasized in her address. There were wives and mothers, heads of colleges and schools, university lecturers, bursars of colleges, teachers, inspectors, government officials, doctors, accountants, research workers of all kinds, writers of books, social and parish workers, J.P.'s and Poor Law Guardians. There was a farmer, an orientalist, an astronomer, and the head of an important department of the Metropolitan Museum, New York. Last, but not least, there was our batch of barristers (they have all had briefs!) and (we mention it with particular pride, since hitherto Girton has been associated with the blue stocking rather than with the buskin) the leading lady of the Old Vic., whose acting has delighted half London for the past two years.

To return to the war: some notes from the *Girton Review* may serve to indicate something of what it meant to those who lived through that time at Girton:

College in war time is without doubt an interesting experience, though in the eyes of many it is a matter for regret that they are missing all that has hitherto been considered characteristic of University life.... Cambridge as a University town is no longer itself. We of the present generation shall never see it as it was, and the old spirit had already become transformed beyond recognition when we began our course....

It seems... impossible at the present time to enter heart and soul into any amusement. There is always a lurking feeling of uneasiness, subconscious perhaps, and unaccounted for, that never allows us quite to forget the happenings of world-wide importance that are taking place not so far away. And now especially in these darkest of days, when the whole country seems to be in suspense, many of us will find it hard to settle down again to the regular life, and the application, more than ever necessary this term. Let us hope that by the time we next leave College, some for good, the problem of the war will be nearer its solution, and some of the tension of waiting relieved.[1]

Nearly eight months were still to pass before the Armistice of November 11th, when thanksgiving services in Cambridge and in the Girton chapel gave expression to intense feelings of relief. Undergraduate invasions followed at Girton, which were suppressed by the proctors, but not before a bonfire had been lighted in the Cloister Court. The *amende honorable* was made on the following evening, when

[1] *Girton Review*, Lent Term, 1918.

a large party of undergraduates came out "to cheer the Mistress, the Staff, and the Students, and held us enthralled by a fascinating and artistically arranged torchlight procession. But the last and greatest excitement of all was the dance which, by the kindness of Miss Jex-Blake, we were permitted to give the raggers—and others—in place of the interrupted celebrations of the previous evenings".[1]

The anxieties and discomforts of the war, and the excitements of the armistice, made these years a time of unusual tension. With the Michaelmas Term, 1919, came a rush of students both to Girton and to the University, and the problems of settling down to work again had to be faced. It was no time for building; wages and prices were still enormously high, and conditions unsettled; yet something must be done to accommodate the candidates anxiously asking for admission. In 1920 a disused army hut was bought, and erected behind the dining hall; this was adapted for use as lecture rooms, while lecture rooms in other parts of the building were adapted for use as living rooms for students. In 1921 a lease was taken of The Grange, a pleasant country house adjoining Girton, which accommodated ten more students.[2] These devices brought the number of students up to 180. Every possible expedient was adopted and the College was uncomfortably crowded, but the problems of a long waiting list of candidates for admission continued as acute as ever. Financial

---

[1] *Girton Review*, Michaelmas Term, 1918.
[2] The Grange was finally purchased in 1926.

difficulties also became acute; the cost of living had risen enormously, and it was difficult to make ends meet, but the improvements needed in drainage and lighting could no longer be postponed owing to labour difficulties with the old systems, and were carried out in 1919. There was nothing for it but to raise the students' fees, which was done by degrees till in 1920 they were fixed at £150 a year. They had never been raised before, since in 1869 they had been fixed at £105.

Dr Cunningham, having stood by Girton throughout the war, resigned the office of Chairman of the Council in 1919, dying shortly after. His place as Chairman was again taken by Mr Berry, who had returned from war service. One of the first events of his new term of office was the Jubilee of the College. The deep sense of relief from the harassing anxiety and misery of the four years of war gave special zest to a meeting of rejoicing and thanksgiving. The celebrations were held at Girton on July 26th. Miss Davies, now aged 89, was unable to attend, but an address signed on the day by past and present students was afterwards received by her with great pleasure. Mr Sedley Taylor, the only other living founder, was warmly welcomed at the garden party with which the celebrations opened. A sympathetic speech was made by the President of the Board of Education (Rt Hon. H. A. L. Fisher), and a vote of thanks was proposed by the Vice-Chancellor of the University (Dr Shipley, Master of Christ's College), and seconded by Mr Berry, as Chairman of the Girton Council. The dinner in the evening was attended by 326 past students, and was memorable for speeches by Mrs Runciman, the Mistress (Miss Jex-Blake), the Senior Student, Miss McClenaghan (speaking for the students in residence), and above all, Miss Lumsden (now Dame Louisa Lumsden). Miss Lumsden spoke with all the fire and idealism to be expected from one of the Girton pioneers, and her presence gave the final touch to the great interest of the occasion. When Miss Jex-Blake rose to speak, the cheering was such as has never been heard in the Hall before or since; bursting out again and again, an expression of warm affection and respect. A delightful Sunday of informal hospitality at the College followed, and was concluded by a service in the chapel, when the sermon was preached by the Rev. Canon Glazebrook. A letter of congratulation from the Principal, Tutors, and Staff of Newnham College, and a Latin letter from the Newnham students, added to the pleasure of these days of rejoicing.

A thank-offering of £376. 5s. 0d., collected on the spur of the moment among the old students assembled at Girton, was given by them to the Mistress, who gave it to the slowly growing endowment of the Old Girtonians' Studentship. Another studentship, of £150 a year, was founded by subscription in 1919 in memory of Miss Ethel Sargant. The year of Jubilee is also memorable for two magnificent gifts. Sir Alfred Yarrow gave £10,000, to be applied during the ensuing twenty years for the encouragement of research in mathematical, physical, and natural sciences;[1] and the trustees of the Rt Hon. Sir Ernest Cassel gave a sum of £1250 per annum for five years, for the encouragement of research (without limitation as to subject) and for increasing the salaries of the staff. (This annual grant was continued for seven years, at the end of which time the capital sum of £25,000 was made over by the Cassel Trustees to the College.) These splendid gifts raised the endowment of research at Girton to quite a different plane. The encouragement afforded to original work has been of immense value, not only as regards the work produced (which has been considerable in volume and it is hoped also in quality), but in setting a high aim before students and teachers, and in enabling a certain number of research students and Fellows to reside in the College, providing an enlargement of the society and a valuable link between students and authorities. The value of travelling Fellowships is also fully recognized; a sum of £200 was collected in 1921 by a Committee of the Girton College Roll for research at a foreign or colonial University, and was awarded to Miss M. G. Tomkinson (a cousin of the founder, Mr Henry Tomkinson) for chemical research at the University of Toulouse. Endowments for scholarships were increased in 1921 by the magnificent bequest of £20,000 from the Countess of Carlisle.

The last public act of Miss Davies's life was to

[1] By Sir Alfred's wish, the capital and interest are being expended annually, in order that scientific research may be developed as rapidly as possible, and the fund will be exhausted by 1940.

send a written reply to the address sent to her from Girton on the occasion of the Jubilee. "The entries attached to the signatures to your address", she wrote, "form a striking record of the work that is being carried on by students of the College. It gives us I think just cause for thankfulness as we look back upon the past fifty years.... We can all rejoice together over what has been achieved, looking forward with hope and trust to the bright promise of the future." Her connection with Girton ceased upon this happy note. She died on July 13th, 1921, in her ninety-second year.

Miss Davies had lived to see women admitted to the suffrage, and she had voted at the first election under the new law in 1919. Women who had passed examinations qualifying for degrees at Oxford and Cambridge voted in this election for the University members. Women were admitted to membership of the University of Oxford in 1919. But Miss Davies did not live to see them admitted in like manner at Cambridge. At the time of her death, the position of the women's Colleges at Cambridge remained precisely as it had been since 1881, with the sole exception that the First and Second M.B. Examinations had been opened to women in 1916.[1] Public opinion as regards women had, however, been profoundly affected by the part they had played in the war; and when a Royal Commission on the Universities of Oxford and Cambridge was appointed in November, 1919, the women's Colleges (though in the case of

[1] The Third M.B. was opened to women in 1922.

Cambridge not officially part of the University) were included within its scope, and two women were appointed among its members—Miss Penrose, Principal of Somerville College, and Miss B. A. Clough, Vice-Principal of Newnham College. But there were many friends of the women's Colleges at Cambridge to whom it seemed that the time was ripe for a spontaneous move from the University. A proposal was accordingly brought before the Senate in December, 1920, to give full membership of the University to members of Girton and Newnham Colleges, and of any other institution for women that might hereafter be recognized by the Senate. This was rejected by 904 votes to 712. A second proposal, to establish a separate University for women, roused very little interest and was rejected by 146 votes to 50; a third proposal, to admit women to membership under certain limitations (the chief of which were exclusion from the Senate, and limitation of their numbers to 500), was rejected by 908 votes to 694. It seems clear, however, that this proposal was supported by a majority of resident members of the University; its rejection was secured by the votes of non-resident members, who were naturally less familiar with the work and character of the women's Colleges. At last in October, 1921, after more than a year of wearisome agitation and discussion, a Grace giving women titular degrees was carried by 1010 votes to 368.

Titular degrees, though helpful to women teachers in general, were no remedy for the difficulties of the women's Colleges. Their work was suffering a real check from the continued exclusion of their teaching staffs from all participation in the work of the University. The failure of the attempt of 1920 to gain admission was a great disappointment, felt by no one more than by the Chairman of the Girton Council, Mr Berry. The women's Colleges have always had strong supporters among those members of the University who were best acquainted with their work, whatever the official attitude may have been.

The Chairmanship of the Girton Council was resigned by Mr Berry in 1921, and he was succeeded by the Master of Emmanuel (Dr Giles), whose wise judgment, prudent counsel, and profound knowledge of the University were used unsparingly for the benefit of the College. Mr Berry was fortunately able to remain on the Council, and continued to render important services. For some time past it had been felt that the time was ripe for a change in the constitution of the College, and it was determined that a Royal Charter should be applied for. The anxieties of the war being over, the Council was able to turn its attention to this problem, and a Committee was appointed on October 25th, 1921, to draw up a scheme for a Charter. This Committee consisted of the Chairman (the Master of Emmanuel), the Mistress (Miss Jex-Blake), the Bursar (Miss Allen), two representatives of the Council (Mrs Adam and Mr Berry), and two Directors of Studies (Miss Cave-Browne-Cave and Miss Thomas).

The work of drafting the Charter was not yet completed when in 1922 Miss Jex-Blake retired from the Mistress-ship. A presentation was made to her by the students, which was recorded in the *Girton Review*:

Miss Jex-Blake then came down into the Stanley Library, where all the staff and students were gathered, and thanked us in a few words for our gift. The favourites among the College songs were sung, and then we parted into two groups to make a way for Miss Jex-Blake to leave the library and as she passed down between us, we cheered her again and again with great enthusiasm, yet we felt it could only be a very faint expression of our grief at losing her, or of our sense of all that she has given to Girton by her character and work. Many of us to whose lot it has fallen to leave Girton at the same time as Miss Jex-Blake feel that the memory of her service there is the chief inspiration we take away with us, and we know that our feeling has been anticipated by generations of students as they said goodbye to Girton and to its Mistress.[1]

Miss Jex-Blake's Mistress-ship was commemorated by the endowment of a Research Fellowship, the money for which was partly subscribed by old students and partly given from the College funds.

[1] *Girton Review*, May Term, 1922.

CHAPTER VII

THE ROYAL COMMISSION
AND THE CHARTER

Miss Phillpotts's Mistress-ship (1922–5). Report of the Royal Commission (1922). The Ordinances of 1923. The Statutory Commission (1923). The Charter (1924). Benefactions to the College. The Fellows' Dining Room.

WITH the resignation of Miss Jex-Blake in 1922, the College entered upon a new period of its history. The retiring Mistress's position in regard to past students was of a character that could not be continued. She was personally acquainted with them all, and had actually been in residence with all except the small number who had left before she entered the College as a Scholar in 1879. Subsequent generations must lose this very special bond, whatever else they gain. Miss Jex-Blake was succeeded by her cousin, Miss Phillpotts (afterwards Dame Bertha Newall), who had entered the College in 1899 as a Pfeiffer Scholar. She held a Pfeiffer Studentship of £50 a year for the years 1903–4 and 1905–6, and served as Librarian from 1906 to 1909. She was therefore well known at Girton. "We feel that you alone could take the place of Miss Jex-Blake", were the words used by the senior student in welcoming her on behalf of the students at the beginning of her Mistress-ship.

Miss Phillpotts's experiences after resigning the

Librarianship at Girton had been of an unusual kind. She spent some years in independent study of the Scandinavian languages, during which she acted as private secretary to Baron Anatole von Hügel, Curator of the University Museum of Archaeology and Ethnology. She was specially interested in the language and customs of Iceland, which she visited six times, attracted thither perhaps as much by her love of adventure as by opportunities for research. A result of these years of work was her book, *Kindred and Clan*, published in 1913, which led to her election to a Lady Carlisle Fellowship at Somerville College, Oxford. In 1916, mid-way through the war, she went to Stockholm, where she remained till 1918 as private secretary to the British Minister, Sir Esmé Howard (now Lord Howard of Penrith). While still in Stockholm she was appointed Principal of Westfield College, London, and after her return to England she entered upon her new duties in 1919. As Principal of Westfield she served on various Boards in the University of London; and she was for some years a member of the Consultative Committee of the Board of Education. Her second book, *The Elder Edda and Ancient Scandinavian Drama*, was published in 1920. The high value of her work had been fully recognized by both English and Scandinavian scholars when in 1921 she was appointed Mistress of Girton. She took up her post in 1922, and held it for only three years; but these years were marked by events of the highest significance—the granting of a Charter to Girton, and the work of the Statutory Commission, which followed on the Report of the Royal Commission on the University. In both of these she bore an important part.

After three years of exhaustive enquiry, the Royal Commission on the Universities of Oxford and Cambridge reported in 1922, recommending a large measure of reorganization in government, work and finance. As regards women at Cambridge their views may be indicated by the following paragraph from their Report:

Although we think it neither possible nor desirable largely to increase the number of women at Cambridge, it is, in our opinion, of the first importance in the national interest that Cambridge should continue to be, alongside of Oxford and the other Universities of the country, a centre of the highest education for women. The advantages which women obtain from the intellectual atmosphere of the place, and from the lectures and laboratories to which they have long been admitted by the "men's University" are very great. It is highly desirable that a limited number of able women should continue to be trained at Cambridge. The University has played a great part in raising and keeping up the level of women's education in the country. A large proportion of the best women teachers in schools and Colleges and also women distinguished in many other professions and walks of life have been trained at Cambridge. It would be a national disaster if the standard of women's education at Cambridge should decline. But in our opinion this result is inevitable in the coming generation if Cambridge is left, for the first time, in the position of the only University in the country where neither women students nor women teachers have the status of membership of the University, and where the teachers, however well qualified, are not eligible for posts or offices in the University, and are excluded from all share in discussions on the organization of teaching.

The latter is now the most serious practical grievance of women at Cambridge; we believe that it is a very real grievance, and that the present conditions tend to diminish the efficiency of the teaching at the women's Colleges.

This was a most emphatic recognition of the work done by the women's Colleges and of their needs; and the Report further included a recommendation that women should be admitted to the University on the same terms as men, subject to certain limitations. It remained to be seen how far the recommendations would be carried out. Four years of suspense followed, while the many and complicated questions dealt with in the Report were being worked out by a Statutory Commission appointed in 1923.

The financial needs of the women's Colleges—a comparatively simple matter—were more promptly dealt with. The Royal Commission found that the funds available for women's education as a whole were "gravely insufficient as compared with the provision for men's education", and "totally inadequate to the needs of the present time". The need for large benefactions was emphatically stated; and the payment of an annual grant of £4000 from public funds was recommended, for the benefit of the women's Colleges at each University, for a period of ten years; one-half of the grant to be earmarked for stipends and pensions. A Grace passed by the Cambridge Senate in November, 1923, set up a Committee to distribute the grant, which was equally divided between Girton and Newnham.

Meanwhile the Grace of 1921 with regard to titular degrees was brought into operation through Ordinances passed by the Senate of the University in 1923. Besides opening titular degrees to women, these Ordinances gave to women students the right of admission to University lectures and laboratories, thus regularizing the usual (though not unbroken) practice of over forty years. The number of women students of undergraduate status was limited to 500. Further Ordinances admitted such students to the University Library on conditions similar to those applying to undergraduates; and women lecturers and holders of the titular M.A. degree were given the same facilities in the use of the library as those enjoyed by graduates. This was a very welcome concession to women teachers; but they were left, as before, to carry on their work in isolation, and outside the organization of the University.

Women students, being largely taught by members of the University (as well as by women lecturers), were scarcely aware of being excluded from anything; but the women lecturers felt increasingly the disadvantages of never being present at the discussion of University schemes of teaching and examining. They fitted in their courses of lectures with the University and intercollegiate lecture lists as best they could, after the publication of these lists at the beginning of the term. This was a serious inconvenience; but it was much more; it meant that the women lecturers had no share in the intellectual life of the University, and it made a great gap in their experience. The difficulty was emphasized by comparison with London and the provincial Universities, where women worked with men as colleagues, sharing freely in the organization and work of teaching, examining, and other University business, as well as in opportunities for advanced work and research. The great attractions thus offered by these Universities tended to draw away from Cambridge some of the ablest among the women educated at Girton and Newnham.

The hopes of the women's Colleges now rested on the Report of the Royal Commission, and on the Cambridge Statutory Commission. The Mistress of Girton, Miss Phillpotts, was the only woman member of this Commission, and on her fell accordingly the responsibility of representing the views and explaining the needs of the women's Colleges at Cambridge. She carried out her anxious and difficult task with the greatest skill and success, thus rendering a service to the cause of women's education which can hardly be estimated too highly. During the whole of her Mistress-ship, and for two years after her resignation of the post, she was deeply engaged in the work of the Commission. Not till 1927, after four years of hard work, were the new Statutes ready for the final approval of the Privy Council and Parliament.

The first two years of Miss Phillpotts's Mistress-ship were largely occupied also with problems of internal government. Some steps had already been taken towards increasing the share of resident members of the staff in the work of the Council. The practice, adopted in 1910, of requesting them to nominate one of their number, who was co-opted by the Council, was carried further, and the number of nominees had been gradually increased till in 1923 four members of the resident staff were serving on the Council, in addition to the Mistress.

The Committee appointed in 1921 to draft a Charter for the College had now finished its labours, and the new Constitution was adopted by the Council in the summer of 1923. An opportunity occurred for making its contents known to past students during the week end of July 28th–30th, when old students were specially invited to the College. The Master of Emmanuel, replying in an after-dinner speech to the toast of the College (as reported in the *Girton Review*), "gave a very clear and interesting account of the proposed Charter...and paid a tribute to the invaluable help in drafting it by Miss Cave, 'which is such', he said, 'that future researchers into the authorship of the College Charter will certainly conclude that it was the work of the person who about the same time became Lord Chancellor of England'".

The Charter, which was granted by the King on August 21st, 1924, constitutes "the Mistress and Governors of Girton College" as a Body Corporate. The provisions of the Charter and Statutes may be roughly summarized as follows:

The Governors consist of:

(1) The Mistress and Staff Fellows (viz. the Vice-Mistress, the Bursar, and such other officers as shall be appointed by the Council to be Staff Fellows).

(2) A number of Research Fellows not exceeding one-quarter of the number of Staff Fellows.

(3) Three representatives of the Cambridge Senate, elected by the Governors of the College.

(4) Six representatives of the Girton College Roll.

(5) A certain number of "additional persons" elected by the Governors.

(6) Eight "Friends of the College", viz. Dame Frances Dove, Miss Kensington, Mrs Latham, Dr Liveing, Dame Louisa Lumsden, Lord Sheffield, Sir Alfred and Lady Yarrow. (No new appointments can be made under this head.)

A Council is appointed by the Governors to conduct the affairs of the College, consisting of the Mistress, Vice-Mistress, Bursar, Staff and Research Fellows as prescribed by the Statutes (ten in all), and eight other members. The Mistress is *ex officio* Chairman of all meetings. On the granting of the Charter, the Master of Emmanuel therefore ceased to be Chairman of the Council, but he consented to hold the office of Vice-Chairman. There is a Visitor, appointed by the Governors; the first Visitor was the Earl of Balfour,[1] Chancellor of the University of Cambridge; he was succeeded by the present Chancellor, the Rt Hon. Stanley Baldwin, M.P.

It will be seen that the Charter places the government of the College mainly in the hands of the

[1] Lord Balfour (who was brother to Mrs Sidgwick, Principal of Newnham College from 1892 to 1910) in 1921 presented an Additional Chancellor's Medal for Law to K. Snell, a student of Girton who came out above the Senior in the Law Tripos for that year, but being a woman was not eligible for the Chancellor's Medal.

Mistress and resident Fellows, with a certain number of representatives of the Cambridge Senate, and of the Girton College Roll, and a small number of people not coming under any of these heads, who are for one reason or another interested in the College and likely to be valuable in its counsels. The governing body is therefore not precisely like that of a constituent College of the University. It has the advantage of being a mixed body, containing, in addition to residents at Girton, members of the University and persons from outside both the College and the University. It is impossible to imagine the work of Girton being carried on without the help of members of the University, so generously given by a long succession since the earliest years, and specially helpful to a newly constituted Council in the days when all its experience lay before it. The Charter has now been in force for eight years, and the new Council has already been called upon to face some serious problems, including the appointments of two Mistresses, and the large addition to the new buildings which will be described in the next chapter.

The financial position of Girton was improved during Miss Phillpott's Mistress-ship by several benefactions. A Scholarship was founded in memory of Miss Emily Davies in 1922 through a gift of £1000 from her niece, Miss Margaret Llewelyn Davies, a former student of the College. Miss Julia Minet in 1924 bequeathed £2000 for the increase of the stipends of the staff, and this was constituted as a fund to be used for "sabbatical years". This has made it possible for Directors of Studies, lecturers, and administrative officers to take occasional leave of absence for nine months, a privilege which has been of great value, giving opportunity for journeys round the world and other interesting travels. Research was encouraged by the gift of two Fellowships of the value of about £143 a year each, founded by Mrs Charles Hancock in 1925, and named by her wish the Hertha Ayrton and Ottilie Hancock Fellowships. About £25,000 was received under the wills of Miss Mary and Miss Amelia Gurney, part of which was bequeathed for the foundation of Classical Scholarships.

The greater events of Miss Phillpotts's Mistressship have been recorded, but there are lesser matters that must also be mentioned, in which she left a very definite mark. It was one of her wishes that the College should be brought into closer touch with Cambridge and with the outer world generally. The facilities open to members of the staff for entertaining friends at Girton were not many, and it is not easy to organize such matters in a large College where service is limited by considerations of expense. Miss Phillpotts contrived a small dining room for the use of Fellows and other members of the staff and their guests. This was done with some ingenuity: the lecture hut erected in 1920 had been placed close to the end of the dining hall where the high table stands; Miss Phillpotts had the lecture room nearest the hall arranged as a dining room, and an entrance made from it to the dais in hall, so that it might serve the purposes of an assembly room before dinner in hall, and of a private dining room. The opportunity of dining and of entertaining guests in privacy and quiet proved invaluable, and the little dining room was immediately much in demand. Miss Phillpotts made another very useful innovation; she built at her own expense a small garage just behind the archway at the front entrance to the College. She was the first member of the Girton staff to have and to drive her own motor-car. Her example was soon followed by others, and garages were erected behind the College for their use. In these as in larger matters she was full of enterprise, swift to take action, undaunted by novelty. She had great opportunities as Mistress, in the Charter and the Statutory Commission; she used them to the full, and yet found time and energy to leave her mark on the College in other ways besides—above all, through the love of learning, the intellectual zeal, which were an abiding inspiration to all who worked with her.

In 1925 Miss Phillpotts found herself obliged to resign owing to the death of her mother, which left her father, now very old and deaf, alone and chiefly dependent on her care. She had held office as Mistress for only three years; but they were years rich in achievement for the College.

.   .   .   .

The story of Girton under Miss Phillpotts as Mistress ends here; but it seems impossible to leave it without adding the short chronicle of her subsequent life. She was elected as a Research Fellow at

Girton in 1925 immediately after she had resigned the Mistress-ship. Two years later, she was appointed Director of Scandinavian Studies at Cambridge. This was a new office, created in consequence of an endowment of £10,000 given to the University for the encouragement of Scandinavian studies. She also had work which took her much to London as she was on the Statutory Commission for the University of London from 1926 to 1928. With all this business on her hands, she continued her own studies, and published in 1931 *Edda and Saga*, in the Home University Library. And all the time she was paying frequent visits to her father, for whose welfare she was responsible, though the care of him in his home at Tunbridge Wells was shared by relations without whose help her various tasks could not have been carried on. As it was, the strain was severe, and made a great demand upon her nervous strength; it was only the swift and masterly methods characteristic of her which enabled her to carry all through. Her services at Stockholm had been recognized by the Government in 1918, when she was given the Order of the British Empire. In 1929 she was made a Dame of the same Order, for her services to scholarship and education.

Dr Phillpotts died in 1930, and in June of the following year Dame Bertha was married to her old friend Professor H. F. Newall, F.R.S., Professor of Astrophysics at Cambridge from 1909 to 1928. She had not long been settled in her new home at Cambridge when the happy years which seemed in prospect were tragically cut short by her death on January 20th, 1932.

The University correspondent of *The Times* said of Dame Bertha that she "brought fame and honour to Girton College and to the whole University by her unrivalled knowledge of the literature and thought of the Scandinavian peoples, and inspired many circles with her fine culture". The impression she made on her colleagues at Girton may be indicated by the following notice in *The Times*, written by a Fellow of the College, Miss J. R. Bacon:

The students of Girton were, as one of them has written, "proud of having a mistress who was eminent in such un-academic ways" as Icelandic travel and small-boat sailing. However brief and rare their actual intercourse with Dame Bertha Newall might be—and her work on the Statutory Commission inevitably circumscribed it, apart from her delicate health—everyone who met her felt the stimulus of her personality. She had a rare power, which was shown in wider spheres also, of swift realization of the needs of the individual or group with whom she was concerned, instantly making them feel that she knew all about them and was really interested in their doings. Having herself had an unconventional education, she had a specially understanding sympathy with "the unusual girl", whose cause she championed when she addressed the Headmistresses' Conference at Leeds in 1929. She never expected anyone to conform to a type, but was ready, and able, to consider every situation on its merits. At the same time she maintained good discipline by her tacit assumption that everyone shared her own high ideals and her own devotion to the college.

The ideal and the service to her college which she herself would, perhaps, most wish to have remembered was her eager encouragement of original research. In her view women had justified their title to "higher education", but, with a few outstanding exceptions, they still needed to prove that they could become great scholars. This was often her theme, and she was herself the strongest argument in favour of it, a living proof of the value of what she preached. It is too soon to measure the harvest of her influence in this field, but many are conscious of the inspiration she gave them, quickening their minds with the infection of her own love of learning. In the sense of irreparable loss which her early death has brought to colleagues, students, and other friends there remains the memory of a vital spirit, "beautiful and swift", a courage that never yielded to pain or weakness, and a mind which gave freely and generously of its great store.

A memorial service for Dame Bertha, arranged by the Vice-Chancellor and attended by him and by many members of the University and of the women's Colleges, was held in the University Church on January 23rd, 1932. A more permanent memorial has been raised in the form of a sum of money subscribed and offered as a benefaction to the University. As a memorial in her own College, the Fellows' Dining Room in the new buildings has been panelled in oak. This dining room is the successor of the temporary building which owed its existence to her care and initiative. The little homely room served its purpose admirably, she was pleased with its success, and the tradition will be carried on by its more solid and handsome substitute. The two memorials seem exactly suitable to Dame Bertha, commemorating on the one hand her love of learning and scholarship, and her wish that Girton should be able to contribute something to the University; and on the other her delightful social gifts, her capacity for friendships, and her wish to add dignity and beauty to Girton. Let us hope that the feelings she inspired will serve to pass on her influence to future generations of students, who will strive towards the fulfilment of her ideals of life and of scholarship.

CHAPTER VIII

THE STATUTES OF 1926, AND THE
NEW BUILDINGS

Miss Major's Mistress-ship (1925–31). The Statutes of 1926. The
new Library and other buildings. The Appointments Board.

"THE summer of 1925 finds all Girtonians at
the mercy of very mixed feelings—the sorrow
of parting with Miss Phillpotts and the joy
of welcoming Miss Major.... Miss Major is an old
and much loved friend of the College. We con-
gratulate ourselves that after a long and distinguished
career at Blackheath, Putney, and Birmingham, she
is willing to return to her own College as Mistress,
and we welcome her with every possible good wish."[1]
In such wise was Miss Phillpotts's successor greeted
at Girton. An old student of the College, she had had
a distinguished career as a teacher, and had since
1911 been Headmistress of King Edward VI School,
Birmingham. She entered upon her duties as Mistress
of Girton at the moment when the great changes
brought about by the Charter were coming into effect,
creating new relations between the Mistress and the
Council, and a new position for the resident staff of
the College. Only a year later, in 1926, relations with
the University were also profoundly changed by the
Statutes consequent upon the Royal Commission. To
Miss Major fell the task of guidance during these

[1] *Girton Review*, May Term, 1925.

critical years of initiation, a task which she was particularly well able to fulfil. Her sound and ready judgment, her wide sympathies, her wit and knowledge of the world, were of the utmost value both within the College and in relation to the University. The Statutes of 1926 and the consequential Ordinances, which gave effect to the recommendations of the Royal Commission, made changes of vital importance in the position of women. Women were made eligible for all teaching offices in the University; and they were admitted to membership of the Faculties set up by the new Statutes for every Tripos, and made eligible for Boards of Faculties. Women also became eligible (in 1927) for all University Scholarships, Studentships and Prizes (except those few where the deed of foundation specifically excludes women). Their admission (as heretofore) to Tripos examinations, and to Diplomas and Certificates, was included in the Ordinances. Women were admitted to courses of research. The course for the Poll Degree examinations remains (with a few exceptions) closed to them, as it has been since 1881; women students are therefore practically all candidates for Honours.

The limitation of women students to the number of 500, already passed by a Grace of 1923, was affirmed in the Ordinances of 1926; this applies only to students of undergraduate standing, and does not include research students.[1] Women cannot be mem-

[1] In October, 1931, the total number of women students not yet qualified for titles of degrees was 436; the total number of men undergraduates was 4746.

bers of the Senate or of the House of Residents, and they are excluded from certain administrative offices. The essential work of the University—teaching and research—is however open to them without restriction; and therefore, although the recommendation of the Royal Commission, that women be entitled to be admitted to membership of the University on the same conditions as men (subject to certain minor limitations), was not carried out, nevertheless great opportunities are now open for developing their work and raising its standard. Those of their lecturers who are members of University Faculties, and of Boards of Faculties, are now able to hear and take part in discussion of the work of the University; and as teachers and examiners they contribute their share towards carrying it out. The new Statutes have been generously interpreted by the University. To begin with, eleven women were appointed as University Lecturers in Faculties, of whom six were Fellows of Girton; a little later, these six were also at various times appointed as members of Boards of Faculties. In 1927 three Fellows of Girton were appointed as Tripos examiners; two members of the College as University Demonstrators; and Miss Phillpotts was made Director of Scandinavian Studies from October 1st, 1927, and Head of a Department under the Faculty of Modern and Medieval Languages. Women graduates are now able to contribute something to the University; and their work has been immensely enlarged in scope and interest, with a corresponding benefit to their Colleges.

The student members of the women's Colleges have already profited considerably by the admission granted in 1927 to University Scholarships and Prizes. Some early successes of Girton students may be noted. A Scandinavian Studentship was awarded to J. I. Young for 1925–7; a Chancellor's Medal for Classics to G. A. Nairn in 1928; a Stewart of Rannoch Scholarship for Sacred Music to D. E. Ling in the same year; a Gibson Spanish Scholarship to J. R. Warren in 1929; grants from the Craven Fund to M. Hartley in 1929 and 1930; the Anthony Wilkin Studentship to M. M. Hunter and a Bell Exhibition to J. H. Lambrick in 1930; the Harness Prize to M. C. Bradbrook in 1931; and in the same year, the Ellen McArthur Prize to F. M. Page. A great stimulus has been given to post-graduate work, and in 1927 there were ten students at Girton working for titular research degrees. In this connection may be mentioned the interesting work done by Miss S. M. Manton, Supervisor in Zoology at the College, who was granted leave of absence for the Lent and Easter Terms, 1929, in order to join the Great Barrier Reef Expedition as a specialist on Crustacea. Miss Manton had for this purpose a University grant of £50 from the Balfour Fund, and a College grant of £250 from the Yarrow Research Fund. It may well be imagined how much the horizon is enlarged by such possibilities, and this enlargement should prove a strong incentive towards a high standard of work at the women's Colleges.

As regards internal organization and relations with

the University, Girton had now made a great advance, with which its material development had not kept pace. For a quarter of a century nothing had been added to the buildings. The debt incurred in 1902 had created a strong prejudice against further building, and in any case nothing of the sort was possible during the war. The peace, as we have seen, led to a rush of students to the Colleges. The temporary expedients adopted to meet the rush were still in force; the military hut bought in 1920 was beginning to wear out—it was both leaky and chilly. The question of library accommodation had also become acute. The Stanley Library, built in 1884, was a beautifully proportioned room, very pleasant to work in. It would be delightful as a library in a good-sized country house; but the needs of the College had long outgrown it. In 1901, when the new dining hall was built, the original hall was fitted up as an additional library, with the help of a benefaction from the then Librarian, Miss Crewdson, and this had sufficed to meet the need for the moment. But by 1927 the two libraries together were quite inadequate, and the books had overflowed into lecture rooms and even passages in various parts of the building.

The ordinary resources of the College were of course quite insufficient to provide for building a new library. There was a larger income and more endowments for scholarships, fellowships, and the like, than in the early days; but the normal and necessary expenditure was far higher. The cost of living had risen immensely since the war, and there were great increases under the headings of salaries and pensions. The cost of tuition had been considerably increased under the new Faculty scheme introduced by the University Statutes. The students' fees had been raised in 1920 to £150, and could not be materially added to. A small fund was available for building, the outcome of a gift to Miss Emily Davies of a sum of 700 guineas presented to her in 1912 as a gift from her friends on the occasion of her Jubilee; this had increased by means of subscriptions and accumulated interest to £5000, and had been presented by her to the College for the purpose nearest her heart, that of building rooms for students. A legacy of £9278 was received in 1927 from Louisa Lady Goldsmid, one of the Founders of the College. But of course these sums alone would not suffice, and far more money was needed.

In March, 1929, therefore, the Council issued an appeal to old students and other friends of the College, which, in spite of the difficulties of the time, met with a wonderfully ready and generous response. An anonymous friend almost immediately offered to defray the cost of a new library, roughly estimated at from £16,000 to £18,000. This went far to ensure the success of the whole scheme; and the Council proceeded to appoint Mr Michael Waterhouse as architect, with Sir Giles Scott as consultant. Mr Waterhouse is grandson to Mr Alfred Waterhouse, the original designer of the College buildings, and son to Mr Paul Waterhouse who designed the Tower wing, the dining hall, and the chapel and woodlands wings; and it is interesting to note that Sir Giles Scott was engaged at the same time on the Girton buildings and the new University Library at Cambridge. The plans drawn up for Girton included a new library, with a reading room on the first floor and storage for books below; rooms for about thirty students;[1] new lecture rooms; and a Fellows' dining room and parlour, replacing the little dining room originated by Miss Phillpotts.[2] Some very necessary alterations to the old buildings were also included, namely, improvements to the Mistress's rooms, with a view to securing greater comfort and privacy, besides additions to kitchens, bathrooms, and so forth. The total cost was estimated at £75,000. A good beginning had been made with the anonymous benefactor's gift, and subscriptions were also given or promised to the amount of £8000. With Miss Davies's building fund the total available by the end of 1929 was about £30,000. A public appeal was launched in October, 1930, at a dinner in London at which the Chancellor of the University (Mr Baldwin) and the Vice-Chancellor (Mr A. B. Ramsay, Master of Magdalene) were among the guests welcomed by the Mistress. Speeches were made in support of the appeal by the Chancellor and by Lord Howard of Penrith (under

[1] Though rooms for 30 students have been added, these only raise the numbers from 180 to 200. The difference represents a very necessary improvement in accommodation.

[2] The small court enclosed by the Fellows' Building and the corridors leading to the dining hall is to be laid out as a garden, the gift of Mr Oswald Lewis in memory of his mother, Eliza Baker, a former student of the College.

whom Miss Phillpotts had served at Stockholm), Sir John Withers, M.P. for the University, Miss Jex-Blake, the Marquess of Crewe, and Lady Henley. Additional subscriptions raised the total to £42,500 —some £30,000 short of what was still needed.

The Council were anxiously considering the possibility of raising this large balance, when the position was entirely altered by a succession of legacies. In 1930, £5000 came to the College under the will of Canon Gamble of Bristol;[1] in 1931 a bequest of something over £4000 was received under the wills of Mr and Mrs Berry,[1] and an additional £4600 from the estates of Miss Mary and Miss Amelia Gurney.[1] In the same year, £19,000 was received as a legacy from Lord Courtney of Penwith.[1] These munificent benefactions, so amazingly well-timed, encouraged the Council to proceed, and the new buildings were begun in the summer of 1931 and carried to completion in the course of 1932. It is hoped that the cost may be met without involving the College in any external debt; but the financial outlook is of course somewhat uncertain, owing to the international financial crisis of 1931 and its far-reaching effects. It is a truism to say that higher education cannot be made to pay its way. As was stated in the Report of the Royal Commission, in private benefaction lies the real hope of future prosperity and development for the Universities. The Government grants were described by the Commission as "a stop gap, not a solution of the problem of University poverty".

[1] See Biographical Index.

Girton, like the University, must look to private generosity for the resources which will enable it to carry on and expand its work.

The anonymous benefactor who gave the money for building the new library has continued to play the part of a fairy godparent, giving in 1931 a further sum of £2000 for the improvement and renovation of the older parts of the building—work which was greatly needed in order to bring the old into line with the new as regards comfort and convenience. The buildings, begun in the later Victorian age, and first planned under Miss Davies's eye, have developed in accordance with her forecast. The new court is almost exactly where she intended it to be; yet the skill of the architects has been able to create a harmonious and dignified group, marrying the modern to the Victorian without discord.

Two years before the new buildings were begun, the College lost, through the death of the Bursar and Vice-Mistress, Miss Eleanor Allen, the last of its residents who had worked in intimate relationship with Miss Davies. Miss Allen had spent her life at Girton in various capacities, and hers was an outstanding influence in the College during the thirty-five years of her service. The College Hall was panelled with oak as a memorial to her, and a commemorative inscription has been incorporated in the decorative panels behind the high table which are part of the design. In these panels may be seen the coat of arms which was granted to the College in 1928. Its charges represent the principal founders of the College; the ermine roundels for Madame Bodichon, the crescents gules for Lady Stanley, the cross for Mr Tomkinson, and the colouring—vert and argent, being the Welsh colours—for Miss Davies, whose family have no arms. These symbols of the past serve to commemorate the founders, and to mark the new status acquired by the College with the grant of a Charter.

Something may here be said of the library to which the new buildings will give a fitting home. It now contains about 29,000 volumes. Its first object is to provide the students with a good working library. It has been gradually built up, partly by means of an annual grant from the College funds (meagre enough in the early days), largely also by means of gifts. Students in residence gave enthusiastically and friends such as Lady Goldsmid helped to lay a solid foundation. Among other donors were George Eliot, John Stuart Mill, Tennyson (1883), and Ruskin (1884), who all gave their works—signed copies in the case of Tennyson. Books were also given by George Henry Lewes, Carlyle, Tom Hughes and the great mathematician Professor Cayley. In 1887 Ruskin gave twenty-four original drawings by Kate Greenaway. Mrs William Morris gave in 1897 three books from the Kelmscott Press, in memory of her husband— *Sidonia the Sorceress*, *The Well at the World's End*, and *Godefroy of Bologne*. About 400 volumes (chiefly English literature) were included in Miss Gamble's bequest of 1885. Mr Justice Wright, for many years a member of the Executive Committee, gave *Punch*

Photo: Palmer Clarke

THE NEW BUILDINGS, 1932

complete to 1883. Original editions of *Lyrical Ballads* and *Cecilia* were given by Mr Maurice Llewelyn Davies in 1930. A bequest of £100 from Mr Berry in the same year was devoted to the purchase of collected editions and expensive books which could not have been bought as a matter of routine. Miss Alice Grüner, an old student of Newnham College, gave a capital sum of £700, the interest on which is devoted to the purchase of Russian and Slavonic books. Other special acquisitions may be mentioned as follows:

The Blackburn Library, received in 1903 under the will of Miss Helen Blackburn—about 400 volumes on the early history of the emancipation of women. This has formed the nucleus of a valuable collection of books on women's work, to which books and papers belonging to Miss Emily Davies have recently been added by the kindness of her niece, Miss Llewelyn Davies, a former student of the College.

The Cowell Library, a collection of about 260 books on Sanskrit language and literature from the library of Professor Cowell (Professor of Sanskrit at Cambridge), given in 1904 by his executors through Miss Ridding, an old student of the College, formerly his pupil.

The Somerville Library, the mathematical library of Mrs Somerville, the distinguished mathematician and astronomer, given by her daughters in 1911.

The Mary Frere Hebrew collection of Semitic and Jewish books and MSS., bequeathed in 1911, and catalogued by Mr H. Loewe.

The Ethel Sargant Botanical collection of books,

papers, and specimens, bequeathed by Miss Sargant in 1918.

Miss Fegan's bibliographical collection, given in 1930 by Miss E. S. Fegan, an old student, Librarian at Girton from 1918 to 1930, now holding an appointment in the Nigerian Educational Service.

Dame Bertha Newall's Scandinavian collection consisting of about 450 volumes received under her will in 1932.

It would be impossible to enumerate all who have given generously both money and books, but the part played by old students in building up the library must be mentioned with special gratitude. Students in residence have also been constant in helping; besides gifts from individuals, the library for many years received regularly from the Bookworms' Society, founded in 1884, books of general literary interest which would not have been bought as a matter of routine.[1] In 1901, when the building debt was pressing heavily on all spending departments, the students organized a Voluntary Library Fund towards the purchase of books, and in 1904 Lady Carlisle gave £100 for the same purpose. The purchase and upkeep of books is necessarily an expensive matter, and the day will never come when benefactions to the library are not warmly welcomed. But it may be said to achieve success in providing the students with what they need; and it manages to keep fairly well abreast with new publications, and even with periodicals, a

[1] This has ceased since about 1917, the Bookworms' Society having before that date degenerated into current fiction.

specially heavy item. The new building will make it easier to display any special treasures that may be acquired.

The women's Colleges, like the University to which they are attached, fulfil not only a special but also a general function. Besides producing scholars and teachers, they also, in the words of the Report of the Royal Commission, "enable a large number of women of special ability, drawn from all classes, to fit themselves for useful and important work in many directions". In the early days of Girton, as we have seen, the demand for teachers was so urgent, the supply so small, that the majority of students were absorbed into the teaching profession. A fair proportion are still so absorbed, and in their case it is not difficult for the College authorities, who are naturally looked to for a supply of highly qualified teachers, to give a helping hand at the outset, and to a certain extent to follow their careers. For students entering upon other occupations, the matter is not so simple; and in 1930 a measure was adopted to meet their needs, and the needs of those employers of labour of all sorts, who want to secure the services of highly educated women. An Appointments Board for women students was created by the joint action of Girton and Newnham, some members of which are appointed by each College, and some by the Cambridge University Appointments Board. The work of such an organization can only be developed slowly, and after careful investigation and testing of ways and means; but with Mrs Oliver Strachey of Newnham College as Chairman, and Miss Sybil Campbell of Girton as Secretary, it is hoped that the Board will prove of great service in the future.

Miss Major, having seen the College well on its way under the new dispensation in relation to the University, resigned the Mistress-ship in 1931. Her previous experience had been different from that of any other Mistress of Girton, since it had lain almost entirely among schools. She had done valuable work for the University of Birmingham while she was Headmistress of King Edward VI School. But her relations with her fellow-mortals would have been something peculiarly her own, whatever her previous experience might have been. "The departure of Miss Major", wrote the Editor of the *Girton Review*, "will be felt by everyone in the College as the loss of a delightful personal friend: others will carry on the very important work she has begun, such as the Women's Appointments Board and the new buildings, but it is difficult to believe that anyone can equal or replace her own particular charm and friendliness." And her successor indicated most happily Miss Major's special gift, when she said, on taking up her office, "Miss Major has made it easy to succeed her".

Of that successor it is too soon to record anything as regards her service to Girton; but a brief mention of her past career may close this chapter. Dr Helen Wodehouse entered the College as a Mathematical Scholar in 1898, and after taking the Mathematical and Moral Sciences Triposes, she was appointed in 1903 as Lecturer in Philosophy at the University of

Birmingham. After eight years she became the first Principal of Bingley Training College, Yorkshire; and in 1919 she was appointed Professor of Education at the University of Bristol. Her published works include *The Logic of Will* (1907); *The Presentation of Reality* (1910); *Nights and Days, and other Lay Sermons* (1916); *God the Prisoner, and other Lay Sermons* (1920); *A Survey of the History of Education* (1924); *The Scripture Lesson in the Elementary School* (1926); besides articles in various periodicals. Girton looks forward to the future of promise which may be hoped for under one of the most distinguished among its past students, and with the newly won opportunities of work within the University.

CHAPTER IX

VARIOUS MATTERS

A room of one's own. Economy and decoration. A dance in 1878. The garden. Methods of conveyance. The gymnasium and gymnastic dress. Acting. Games. Societies. The *Girton Review*. Students' Representative Committee. Labour-saving arrangements. The Roll. Summer Sessions. Reading rooms in Cambridge. The Chapel. Memorials and Portraits. Curators' Committee. Gifts to the College.

THE story of the College has been told in outline down to the end of the year 1932. It remains to notice various matters of lesser importance, which for Girtonians may be worthy of record, but cannot conveniently be included in the main story.

An American traveller who visited Girton in 1879 was much impressed by the fact that each student had "*a room to herself*; in the lower stories, *each has two rooms*". The new buildings then in progress, as he remarked, would accommodate nineteen additional students. "This new building is to cost £8000 (40,000 dols.)—a sum for which an American college would have accommodated forty or fifty pupils. But it would have been by crowding them together; and Girton may well forgo elegancies and even comforts for the sake of the health and privacy of its students."[1] In the first "programme" drawn up by Miss Davies for the College in 1868 she had written:

[1] *Cambridge Chronicle*, February 1st, 1879.

Each student will have a small sitting room to herself, where she will be free to study undisturbed, and to enjoy at her discretion the companionship of friends of her own choice. Of all the attractions offered by the College life, probably the opportunity for a certain amount of solitude, so necessary an agent in the formation of character, will be the one most welcomed by the real student.

Solitude is not exactly what one thinks of as the special attraction of Girton nowadays. But Miss Davies was right. Girls in her day suffered from the want of it; they were expected to pass practically all their time in the family circle, without freedom to pursue the occupations or to entertain the friends of their own choice. This freedom has been won so completely that the need for at least one room for each student is now taken for granted. Miss Davies went so far as to insist on a bedroom and sitting room for each, in some cases divided only by curtains, but for the most part separate rooms. This was in her eyes a necessity, if women were to have the real advantages of university education. As for the "elegancies and comforts" alluded to by the American visitor, she did not care for such things herself, and she was determined to keep them subordinate to the main object of creating a College. The addition that he saw being built brought the number of students up to fifty-eight. The process of growth was slow and laborious. Nowadays, though financial troubles loom large, the need for women's education is so thoroughly established that funds are actually easier to raise than they were in the last century, when money was plentiful, but hardly anyone approved of Colleges for women. Miss Davies, though she planned things on a large scale, sternly repressed any tendency towards unnecessary spending. In 1875, when the first block of buildings had already been in existence some three years, Madame Bodichon, who had for some time been urging that the walls should be papered and painted, offered to provide for the decoration of the Mistress's room and the reception room. With the help of her friend, Miss Gertrude Jekyll (the famous gardening expert), she also chose a scheme of colouring for the work to be done throughout the whole building. But no; this might cost £300, and only £70 would then be left in the bank. "It does not seem as if·this work was of urgent necessity", wrote Miss Davies. "Of course the place looks unfinished, but that is not altogether a disadvantage. It brings home to people that we have no money. When everything looks smooth and nice, it does not occur to people that it is not paid for. And for the students it is not amiss I think to have a reminder that the place did not grow up of itself without any trouble."

Unfortunately Madame Bodichon's illness in 1877 made it impossible for her to visit Girton again, and she was never able to supervise the decoration of the building. At last in 1879 something was done. "Lady Stanley is going to give us a high chimney piece with blue and white china on, for the Dining Hall, besides having the walls colour-washed this vacation", wrote Miss Marks (afterwards Mrs Ayrton) to Madame Bodichon. "It will be delightful to see something different from those hideous walls when we dine." Alas, the gift proved disappointing. "The Dining hall has been painted," she wrote a month later, "and hideously done. It has a kind of reddish brown dado, and cream colour at the top, and the dado is varnished! It looks like a huge bathroom. I think it is *much* uglier than before, and now we have no hope of its being made better." The reddish brown dado, and the varnish, were no doubt chosen for their wearing qualities, and the tradition then started was carried on relentlessly for many years.

Small and poor as the College was, there was plenty of life and gaiety in it. A letter written by Miss Marks to Madame Bodichon in 1878, when the students were only about forty in number, gives the impression of a cheerful family party, all the members throwing themselves eagerly into the preparations for a dance, enjoying the makeshifts, and proud of producing much out of little:

The party went off magnificently. Everyone enjoyed it vigorously, and all danced as if fatigue could never by any possibility be known to them....All day the College was in a state of essentially feminine ferment, i.e., everyone was putting finishing touches to dresses....At half past eight everything was in the most cheerful state of readiness, the hall[1] had chairs, and the big blue china things set round a blazing fire, the dining hall[2] was decorated with a big Indian

[1] The entrance hall by the old front door, under the clock.

[2] The old dining hall, later used as a library, and now to become a lecture hall.

embroidered bed quilt, and Indian shawls arranged in patterns on the walls, and the floors were beautifully waxed and had a border of blue carpet taken up from somewhere else. The two lower corridors were lighted up and the rooms all thrown open. The top one was not to be shown because its curtains had been taken down, and carpets taken up, to assist in decorating other parts. . . . The rooms that were used besides the hall were the two reading rooms (one of them the old laboratory) fenced round with couches and easy chairs, and delightfully cool and restful after dancing, the classical lecture room for supper, the pantry, turned by Miss Bernard's magic hand into a "green parlour", and last, and by far the most charming, the kitchen, in which tea and refreshments were handed round. It was lighted up with quantities of candles in brass candlesticks, the beautiful light wood dressers, which you must know, were covered with plates, altogether it was the most picturesque room in the house.

Supper began at half-past ten, and the Cotillon was danced at about half-past eleven. It went off beautifully. . . .

Carriages had been ordered for a quarter to twelve, but people *would* not go, and at last at half-past one, Miss Bernard had to turn a number of gentlemen out, who would keep begging for one more dance. Doesn't that look as if they enjoyed it?

During the evening Mr McAlister showed the Geissler tubes in the Natural Science lecture room. They are tubes full of different kinds of gases and substances, which when lighted up by electricity show beautiful colours.

Everyone was much surprised at students' rooms being thrown open to the public. It appears that in Cambridge it is supposed that Girton is a most mysterious place, and that in everything belonging to it there is much more than meets the eye. The rooms, and indeed the whole place, were very much admired, and I took advantage of the occasion to let two or three people know that we wanted money for building.

The tall brass candlesticks used on this occasion to light the kitchen were a feature of College life until 1919, when electric light was put in. Every student had two, so plenty of them could be collected for great occasions. In Miss Welsh's time the Stanley Library—built, as it will be remembered, in 1884, the year before she became Mistress—was used as a ballroom when she gave a dance, as she usually did in alternate years. On these occasions, the candles were set in rows on top of the tall bookcases round the walls, and the effect was very gay and pretty. The Stanley Library was always by far the most attractive room in the College. It had the advantage of being lined with books, a most satisfactory form of decoration; there was no question here of a brown varnished dado.

The outer surroundings of the College were for a good many years bleak and uninviting. The American observer of 1879, already quoted, remarked that the grounds were "scanty and rough.... There is almost nothing that is attractive in the external appearance of the establishment". There was of course no money available for the garden. "I am quite of your opinion", wrote Miss Metcalfe to Madame Bodichon, "that it is useless to give gifts to a garden so utterly uncared for.... I am certainly not tall, but the weeds are taller than I am.... I cannot tell you how my heart sinks whenever I see the dismally uncared-for state of the garden, front and back." Miss Metcalfe and her sister, with the help of friends, got together a sum of over £400 which in 1881 was spent under her direction on improving the garden and grounds. Another great benefactor to the garden was Miss Welsh, who as Garden Steward devoted a great deal of time and attention to it. When she was designing the planting of the grounds, she used to go up to the top of the tower in order to study the lie of the land. Her tall dignified figure was often seen walking round Woodlands, with Bonwick the gardener in attendance. The trees and shrubberies were kept in excellent order through her constant care in thinning them. It was she who planted the fine yew hedges near the pond, and the lovely honeysuckle walk. The garden suffered during the war, when labour was hard to get, and flowers had to give place to vegetables; but the produce went a long way to relieve the difficulties caused by the rationing of food, and the profits on the pigs helped to pay wages. The garden is now managed by a professionally trained woman appointed as Garden Steward. A delightful feature of recent years is the garden made by Miss K. T. Butler (Director of Studies in Modern and Medieval Languages) beside the pond. Miss Cave (Director in Mathematics) has also done much for the garden, especially by the introduction of flowers among the trees and shrubs of Woodlands. In 1926 the acquisition of the Grange added its very pretty garden to the grounds of the College.

Many generations of students will remember

Bonwick, the head gardener. It is pleasant to note how many of the indoor and outdoor staff of the College have given it long years of loyal service. The Council recorded in 1931 the completion of fifty years' service by William Lingley, the engineer, who retired in September, 1932. His knowledge of the gradual growth of the buildings was invaluable to the architects and engineers of the last extension. Walter Crane, houseman, and Lena Butler, housemaid, have recently retired after spending the greater part of their lives in the service of the College; Rachel Asplin, who came three months later than William Lingley (whom she afterwards married), continues to help at times of stress. Girton still enjoys the services of King, who entered its employment as houseman in 1895. Others who have not yet completed their second decade of service continue the tradition, and are invaluable in promoting the smooth working of domestic arrangements.

A pair of cottages was built in 1925 by the gate on the Girton Road, to house men employed in the College; another cottage at the entrance by the Hospital forms part of the building scheme of 1932. Bicycle sheds and garages have been built at various spots, as need arose. In early years, the students were conveyed to and from lectures in "flys" provided by the College; it seems necessary now to explain that these were horse-drawn carriages hired from Moore's, and later from Cox's, livery stables in Cambridge. As these vehicles became extinct, their place was taken by taxis, and finally by omnibuses. Miss Phillpotts's example in having a motor-car of her own was quickly followed by other members of the staff. All this meant that the College came into much closer contact with Cambridge, and Cambridge itself came nearer as houses spread along the Huntingdon Road; which road was vastly improved by the avenue of elms planted at Miss Welsh's instigation in the 'nineties, the cost being borne by past students of Girton.

Facilities for games and athletics were introduced gradually. Lady Rich planned to give a gymnasium; her death, which occurred suddenly in 1874, prevented this, but her intention was carried out by the Committee with the help of her cousin Mr Tomkinson. The building was sometimes used for racquets, sometimes as a gymnasium. Miss Davies was concerned as to the dress to be worn for gymnastics. "I have come to the conclusion that we had better not prescribe one dress," she wrote to Madame Bodichon, "as there seem to be so many harmless varieties, but to make it subject to the approval of the Mistress, and I am inclined to make essential these points—full trousers to the ankle, skirt, blouse or tunic to the throat with long sleeves and two or three inches below the knee." Miss Metcalfe was inclined to allow more freedom. "The gymnasium will give us trouble," she wrote to Madame Bodichon, "but I think the time for sumptuary laws has past, and though I think we can dictate where it shall be worn, I do not see that we can say what shall *not* be worn until we find something really unfitting and objectionable.... Is it worth while to irritate the students at every point with the Committee's *authority?...* It seems to me very different from the acting in tight-fitting men's dress. That was for no purpose beyond *exhibiting* themselves for amusement. This is for a purpose which cannot be carried out in the usual woman's dress, and I think it is in our province to say it shall not be worn outside the gymnasium walls."

Miss Metcalfe was here referring to the difficulty about acting in men's dress which had occurred at Hitchin. Her letter and Miss Davies's bring vividly before us the change of fashion brought about in women's dress by the war. Before the war, no woman was ever seen in man's dress, except on the stage. Riding astride came into fashion to a certain extent about 1912 or so; but it was the war which made it possible for women to appear in trousers, skirts being quite out of place for such war work as cleaning railway carriages, and the like. Public opinion would have been inexpressibly shocked by anything of the sort in 1874; and Miss Metcalfe took a liberal view when she told Madame Bodichon that she thought the students should be allowed to choose their gymnastic dress so long as they wore it only within the gymnasium.

As regards acting, the most important achievement at Girton was the *Electra* of Sophocles, performed by the students in 1883, as recorded in Chapter v. A Dramatic Society came into existence in 1882. The *Electra* was given in the gymnasium; other performances took place in the old dining hall; now, in its new guise as a lecture hall, to be fitted with a stage suitable for acting as well as for lecturing; so completely have the actors established their claims.

Outdoor games were gradually established at Girton; and in this, as well as in intellectual matters, Dame Louisa Lumsden and the schoolmistresses of her generation were pioneers. She introduced gymnastics and games at St Leonards School. Lawn tennis began to be played at Girton in 1873, and matches, both singles and doubles, were soon played against Newnham. Miss Gadesden, a student at the College from 1879 to 1883, did much to stimulate interest in the game; more grass courts were made at the students' request, and in 1883 Miss C. A. Scott (the first woman wrangler) presented a silver challenge cup for the doubles matches with Newnham. Various other cups have been subscribed for or presented. The first match with the Oxford women's Colleges was played in 1882, when perpetual challenge badges were presented by Mr E. N. Buxton (a member of the Girton Committee) and Mr A. Johnston. Mr Buxton's is a silver owl holding a racquet in its beak; Mr Johnston's a gold medal with the following inscription on the case:

Presented by the Corporation of London to Andrew Johnston, Verderer, on the visit of H.M. Queen Victoria to Epping Forest, 6th May 1882, and by him as a Perpetual Challenge Badge for Oxford v. Cambridge Ladies Four-Handed Lawn Tennis. Woodford, 29th June, 1882.

A Racquet Club was formed in 1875, and existed till 1886 or soon after. A Hockey Club was formed in 1890; year matches began to be played in 1891, and matches between Newnham and Girton about the same time. Cups were presented or subscribed for, including one given in 1898 for matches with the Oxford women's Colleges, by two sisters, I. P. Scott of Newnham, and A. D. Scott of Somerville—both Old Roedeanians, and nieces of Mr C. P. Scott of the *Manchester Guardian*, whose wife was the Girton pioneer, Rachel Cook. Other matches are played, with Holloway College (since 1894), Past Girtonians (since 1895), and various ladies' clubs and girls' schools.

A Golf Club was formed in 1891, and it was a source of some pride that the Girton grounds were large enough to contain quite a good little course; but this came to an end when the new buildings of 1902 encroached on the course. Cricket has been played from time to time, and a Challenge Cup was presented by L. B. Legg of Newnham in 1897 for intercollegiate matches, but the game has not taken permanent root. A swimming bath was given by Miss Julia Lindley and Mrs Durham, with some help from old students, in 1900. A Swimming Club was started in 1901, a Boat Club in 1906. A Bicycle Club was formed in 1894, when bicycling became possible for women with the invention of the safety bicycle with two low wheels of equal size. The introduction of this new fashion was carefully supervised; students were obliged to pass a test before they might ride to Cambridge, and they were not allowed to ride in the town. These restrictions were of course removed when women bicyclists ceased to be stared at as an extraordinary novelty. Conventions changed slowly, especially as regards young women. The first women students were chaperoned to lectures by an older woman; this was in accordance with the customs of the time, and was required by the authorities of the men's Colleges (who naturally have their own views) as well as by the public opinion of Cambridge. Cambridge society took strict views in these matters; Mrs Adam has recorded that in the 'eighties it was with some difficulty that she secured leave to join the C.U.M.S. orchestra, after Miss Welsh had made careful enquiry in Cambridge as to whether this would be considered proper; and a chaperon was required at rehearsals (women never played in orchestras in those days). On the other hand, students were encouraged to join the C.U.M.S. chorus, for which their fees were paid by the College. Restrictions were of course relaxed as public opinion changed on the subject. To ignore it would have been—and would still be—fatal to the prosperity of the College. And the public opinion that has to be consulted is of a very special kind and is applied to very special circumstances; Cambridge, a small county town in a sparsely inhabited country-side, has had grafted on to it a University containing nineteen residential Colleges (besides the two women's Colleges) and over 4000 undergraduates; and the result is a structure which, though it seems normal to its inhabitants, resembles nothing else in the world, with the sole exception of Oxford.

Of what may be called indoor societies at Girton,

one of the most active used to be the Fire Brigade, founded in December, 1878, by three students, H. Marks (Mrs Ayrton), M. Parker (Mrs Carmichael) and G. E. M. Jackson (afterwards Junior Bursar of the College). Miss Jackson, having seen some haystacks burning near the College (this makes one realize its rustic surroundings), thought it would be well to take precautions against fire. The students accordingly organized a Brigade with the help and advice of Captain Shaw (the Captain of the London Fire Brigade immortalized in *Iolanthe*). In the earlier years, practically all the students belonged to it, and it served the purpose of collecting them at fixed spots, which would have been very useful if the emergency had ever occurred; but it never did, *mirabile dictu!* for the students' rooms were all lit by candles and oil lamps.

As to other societies, their name is legion. The Classical Club was started in 1884 by Miss Janet Case and Miss Zimmern, and students in other subjects followed suit and started clubs in connection with their Tripos work. A Debating Society was formed in 1875; the first debate with Newnham was held in 1885; the first with Oxford in 1892. Other debating societies have risen and fallen from time to time, and debates have been held with societies from some of the men's Colleges. A Musical Society was formed in 1871; and music has benefited by the existence of the chapel organ, given by past and present students and friends, in 1910. Mrs Rawlings subscribed £200 towards the cost; Mr Sedley Taylor gave £100 and also an Organ Scholarship of £50 a year for three years. A Musical Scholarship was founded in 1914 with a gift of £2300 from Miss S. A. Turle, and through a legacy under her will a second scholarship was established in 1924. The new buildings of 1932 contain a sound-proof room for practice, adjoining the chapel, primarily for the benefit of students working for the Mus.Bac. examinations.

Since early days, religious and philanthropic societies have played a large part in the College, and have carried their activities into the after-life of students. A Prayer Meeting was started by Miss C. L. Maynard about 1873 which was later merged in the Student Christian Movement. The Women's University Settlement was established in 1887 in Southwark by former students of Newnham and Girton, the first institution of the kind to be worked by women; it is maintained principally by University women from Oxford, Cambridge and London, and has a local Committee at Girton. When the war came, a Social Service Club was initiated at Girton by the Christian Union in order to link the various societies together; this included the Women's Suffrage Society, the Women's University Settlement Committee, the Women's University Missionary Settlement, the National Union of Women Workers, the Workers' Educational Association, the Society for Providing a Village Nurse (for Girton village), and the York Street Girls' Club, as well as the Christian Union. The war also gave rise to the formation of a Girton and Newnham Hospital Unit, organized as part of the Scottish Women's Hospital. An initial sum of £1000 was raised among Girton and Newnham students, past and present, for the equipment of this hospital; they kept it going during the war, and a Girton and Newnham bed endowed in 1923 at the Royal Free Hospital for Women in Gray's Inn Road remains as a permanent outcome of this effort. In 1919 an annual Social Service Week was organized in the University, in connection with Talbot House and the Women's University Settlement, by means of which men and women students are enabled to spend a week in London during the Christmas vacation, and to see something of Juvenile Labour Exchanges, Play Centres, Care Committee work, and so forth; usually ending with a visit to the Old Vic!

It will be seen that philanthropy and amusement are both well provided for at Girton, and the choice among so many interests, while demanding much self-control from the modern student, gives great opportunities, of which she makes full use. The doings of these various societies are recorded in the *Girton Review*, founded in 1882 by Miss Jex-Blake, Miss Gadesden, Miss E. Macleod, and some other students. This is invaluable as a source of information, and it is much to be hoped that it will continue to provide not only a record, but a commentary on contemporary events, for the benefit of future historians of the College.

It will readily be understood that with this great variety of organizations within the College, the responsibility devolving upon the Senior Student has much increased. The Senior Student was originally the student whose name came first on the marking roll. Since 1906, she has been elected by the second, third, and fourth year students; and a Students' Representative Committee has been formed, consisting of the Senior Student, with members from every year. The College must in fact become more highly organized as it grows. Other changes are due to the necessity for saving labour; the little baths in students' bedrooms were done away with long ago; bathrooms have been multiplied to an extent that would have shocked Miss Davies; fixed basins have been put in the gyp wings, and in the new buildings, even in the bedrooms! Since 1909 afternoon tea has been served in hall, as are all the other meals; cups of tea are no longer as of old taken round to the students' rooms. Miss Marks's description of the kitchen in 1878 conjures up a vision of a cottage kitchen with a dresser and a kettle on the hob; the kitchen of to-day could not by any possibility be adapted as a picturesque sitting-out room for a dance; it is full of steam cookers, machines for peeling potatoes and washing plates, and the like. The College has become mechanized; it has lost some charms, but it has certainly gained others, and it is warmer, more comfortable, and better managed as regards cooking and catering. What may be called the standard of housing is on the whole improved. The lecturers have better accommodation, and the students' rooms are better furnished; but pressure on space has led to the introduction of a certain number of bed-sitting rooms, thus departing to a slight extent from Miss Davies's ideal of a bedroom and a sitting room.

The Girton College Roll, which keeps past students in touch with the College, has already been described.[1] Past students have the privilege of taking occasional meals in the College, and of residence during the Long Vacation under certain conditions. In the summers of 1907 and 1911, vacation courses for past students were held, with the help of a contribution of £100 from an anonymous donor. Dame Bertha Newall bequeathed £100 to the College, which in accordance with her wish will be used for a third Old Students' Session in 1933. Others have been allowed to use the College for special sessions from time to time during the Long Vacation, including the Modern Churchmen's Union, the Vacation Term for Biblical Study, the Italian Summer School, the Classical Association, the Drapers' Chamber of Trades, the Institute of Industrial Welfare Workers, and many others. Members of the British Association stayed at Girton when the Association met in Cambridge in 1904; papers were read at this meeting by four old students, Miss Constance Jones, Mrs Ayrton, Miss Hardcastle, and Miss Cave.

A useful offshoot from the College deserves mention, namely, the Reading Rooms in Cambridge, established primarily for the benefit of students attending lectures and examinations in Cambridge. The need for some haven of this sort was early felt, and was first met by an arrangement for students to

[1] See Chapter vi.

join the Cambridge Ladies' Reading Room in the Market Place. When independent arrangements became desirable, as the College grew in numbers, rooms were rented at 5 Bene't Street, and later in Falcon Yard; till in 1920 the lease was taken of a house in St Edward's Passage. A good-sized lecture room is available there, which has proved useful to lecturers giving courses attended by Newnham students and by undergraduates as well as by Girtonians.

The chapel is a comparatively recent institution, having been built in 1902; but services had been held at the College since 1881, when they were instituted through the kindness of Dr A. H. Cooke of King's, who came regularly and conducted them in the dining hall, till his appointment in 1899 as headmaster of Aldenham School. The chapel is used for morning prayers, usually said by the Mistress, and for Sunday services; there is no chaplain, but arrangements are made for clergy of various denominations to conduct services. A Chapel Committee consisting of students representing various shades of opinion co-operates with the Mistress in making these arrangements; this was due to the initiative of Miss Phillpotts, who also introduced the custom of the lessons being read by students. A special service is held annually on the Sunday nearest to October 16th, Founders' Day, at which the names of founders and benefactors are recited. The oak panels in the chancel were carved by Miss Meyer and Miss Carthew and other old students under their direction; the panelling was carried round the rest of the interior in 1926 as a memorial to Miss Meyer. The carved oak railing dividing the chancel from the body of the chapel was provided out of a fund left by Miss Meyer and administered by Miss Carthew. The chapel contains memorials to Miss Davies, Miss Welsh, Miss Constance Jones, and others connected with the College.

The founders of Girton are commemorated by an annual lecture endowed in 1927 by means of a gift of £500 from an old student, Miss Amy Lawrence. The lecturer is chosen by the Mistress, and may discourse upon any subject. The first lecture was given in the Lent Term of 1928 by the Master of Trinity, Sir Joseph Thomson; and the subject, *Beyond the Electron*, was treated in such a way as to impress on the majority who are ignorant of electrons something of the inspiration and adventure attaching to scientific research. It was a high privilege for Girton that the series of Founders' Memorial Lectures should begin so brilliantly.

The College owns other memorials in the shape of portraits, of which the principal are as follows:[1]

MISS DAVIES, by R. Lehmann.

MADAME BODICHON, by Samuel Laurence, given by her niece, Milicent Lady Moore.

MR TOMKINSON, by Mrs Macleod after Hon. John Collier, given by Mrs Macleod and Miss Leveson.

[1] Where no donor is mentioned, these were subscribed for by past students.

LADY STANLEY OF ALDERLEY, by Miss M. Hawkins,
    after W. B. Richmond, given by her son, Lord Sheffield.
MRS LATHAM (Miss Bernard), by F. Dodd.
MISS WELSH, by Sir John Lavery.
MISS CONSTANCE JONES, by Sir John Lavery.
MISS JEX-BLAKE, by Herman Herkomer, given by Mrs
    Jex-Blake.
MISS PHILLPOTTS, by H. Somerville.
MISS MAJOR, by Mr Sleator, after Sir William Orpen.
MISS GAMBLE, by Chalon—part of the Gamble bequest.
MRS AYRTON, by Helena Darmesteter, given by Mrs
    Ayrton Gould.

A small water-colour portrait of Lady Stanley by
her son-in-law, Lord Carlisle, was given in 1911
by Lady Henley. The first three Mistresses, Mrs
Manning, Miss Shirreff and Mrs Austin, are represented by small portraits, and there are also a number
of small portraits of other benefactors and old
students of distinction. These have been collected
together and hung by the Curators' Committee,
which was set on foot in 1927 in order to supervise
the arrangement and care of pictures, works of art,
antiquities, and so forth; with power to accept or
refuse gifts; and the further duty of supervising
internal decorations and amenities generally. This
Committee also gathered together a number of en-
gravings of Rome by Piranesi, previously scattered
in lecture rooms; the collection was increased by
gifts from Miss Carthew and Miss Murray. It is
hoped that the new buildings will make it possible
to exhibit antiquities and objects of art to better

advantage. Among such things owned by the College are a number of Anglo-Saxon and Roman objects found in 1881 and 1886 in the course of building and draining operations, when it became apparent that the site of the College was occupied in the second century A.D. by a Roman dwelling house, the exact situation of which has not been determined, and was later used as a cemetery by a group of Anglian settlers who seem to have come from the direction of the Cam valley and made their home where the village of Girton now stands. Most of the objects found are in the Cambridge Museum of Archaeology and Ethnology; among those preserved at Girton is a spirited representation in stone of a lion's head.[1] The College also owns a beautiful set of Tanagra figures presented in 1902 by an old student, Hon. Evelyn Saumarez (Hon. Mrs Wood), whose father, Lord de Saumarez, collected them when at Athens as Secretary to the British Legation; and a number of Egyptian antiquities presented, some by Miss Crewdson and some by Miss Meyer. It may be noted that the three marbles hitherto kept in the Stanley Library—the bust of Dante, the figure of Lorenzo dei Medici after Michael Angelo, and the copy of Canova's *Psyche* were all part of Miss Gamble's bequest, as was also the relief of Pandora and Mercury after Flaxman, in the entrance hall, and the original model of Chantrey's *Sleeping Child*, which was given to Miss Gamble by Lady Chantrey. The

[1] *The Anglo-Saxon Cemetery at Girton College*, by E. J. Hollingworth and M. M. O'Reilly.

original drawings for *Wayside Songs of Tuscany*, by Francesca Alexander, were given to Girton by Ruskin in 1887; probably through Miss Anna Lloyd. The cast of the head of Hera in the Stanley Library was given by Dr Montagu Butler, Master of Trinity; the cast of figures from the Parthenon frieze by an old student, Miss Alice Barlow. The embroidered wall hangings in the Reception Room, worked by Lady Carew, were set in oak panelling designed by Sir Edwin Cooper (whose daughter had been a student at Girton), and given, with the furniture of the room, in 1923 by Annie Viscountess Cowdray in memory of Lady Carew, whose portrait hangs in the room. Such gifts are a great encouragement to all attempts to improve the decoration and amenities of the buildings, and the safeguarding of them is a privilege which in itself should contribute something to the educational value of the College.

The College, as befits its origin, owns some memorials of distinguished women unconnected, or only slightly connected, with it. The gold medal presented by the Royal Astronomical Society to Caroline Herschel was given by her niece, Lady Hamilton Gordon, whose sister, Lady Lubbock, is an old student, and was formerly mathematical lecturer at Girton. An interesting portrait of Caroline Herschel was given by an old student, Miss Hardcastle, in 1932. Mary Somerville's mathematical library has already been mentioned; a bust of her was given by Miss Frances Power Cobbe, and a portrait sketch by Samuel Laurence was also given by Lady Stanley in

1884. Another portrait by Samuel Laurence, that of George Eliot, was given by Mr Maurice Llewelyn Davies. The portrait of Miss Anna Swanwick, distinguished in her day as a translator of Greek and German literature, was given in 1920 by Mrs Elmslie, wife of the painter.

It is impossible to enumerate all the gifts which have been received. In this, as in other matters, it is impressive to find how many have cared for Girton, and thought of its needs. It is the work of innumerable hands and minds, of which any record must necessarily be incomplete; and the result we see is a living and growing institution. Old students may be shocked by changes in the face of things, and the founders of the College, could they return to see it, would be amazed, and perhaps shocked also, at its magnificence compared to the little block of 1873. But it is to be hoped that they would feel that something has been achieved towards the realization of their vision. Much still remains to be done; but the educated woman is no longer a solecism, and the ideals of life placed before women in general are of a wider scope and cast in a larger mould than ever before. For Girton to press on in raising these ideals is the best tribute that can be offered to the founders.

BIOGRAPHICAL INDEX

This index is intended to provide a record of founders and benefactors and others of importance to Girton, including some distinguished old students commemorated at the College, in the chapel or elsewhere. Limitations of space make it necessary that the record should be brief; and in many cases the names of old students and others commemorated by scholarships and other endowments have not been included, if their life-work was not especially connected with Girton. Those whose names are marked with an asterisk have been more fully noticed in *Emily Davies and Girton College*.

I have to thank many correspondents who have supplied me with information, among whom I may name Mrs Adam, Mrs Ball, Miss Buchanan, Miss Jex-Blake, Mr Minet, Miss Moyers, Mr A. Hamilton Smith, and Miss Sturge.

ADAM, JAMES, 1860–1907; Classical Scholar of Caius College, Cambridge; Classical Tripos, Part I, Cl. I, Div. 1, 1882; Part II, Cl. I, with distinction in Pure Scholarship, Ancient Philosophy, and Philology, 1884; Fellow and Classical Lecturer of Emmanuel College, 1884; Tutor, 1890; Senior Tutor, 1900. Married in 1890 Adela Marion Kensington (student of Girton, 1885–9; Classical Tripos, Part I, Cl. I, 1888; Part II, Cl. I, 1889, with special distinction in Philosophy; sister to Frances Kensington, *q.v.*). Author of editions of Plato's *Republic*, *Protagoras* (in conjunction with Mrs Adam), and other works. Lecturer at Girton, 1885–1907. Representative Member of Girton College appointed by the Senate, 1892–1902.

ADAMS, JOHN COUCH, 1819–92, P.R.A.S., F.R.S.; Lowndean Professor of Astronomy, 1858–92. In 1845 he inferred the existence of an unknown planet (Neptune, discovered by Galle in 1846) from the perturbations of Uranus. One of the first Members of Girton College appointed by the Senate, 1880. *See* SOMER-VILLE, MARY.

ALFORD, HENRY, 1810–71; Scholar of Trinity College, Cambridge; 8th Classic and 34th Wrangler, 1832. Dean of Canterbury, 1857–71. Editor of the Greek Testament (1849–61). He also published sermons, poems, hymns, translations from the Classics, etc. He did much for the restoration of the cathedral buildings at Canterbury, and for the encouragement of music. An original member of the Executive Committee of The College for Women (afterwards Girton College), 1867.

ALLEN, ELEANOR MARGARET, 1867–1929, daughter of Robin Allen (Secretary to the Trinity House); student at Girton, 1889–93; Modern Languages Tripos, Aegrotat, 1893; Acting Junior Bursar at Girton, 1894; Librarian and Registrar, 1895–7 and 1903–6; Junior Bursar, 1897–1902; Vice-Mistress, 1916–23; Bursar, 1906–29. Miss Allen bequeathed £1000 to the College for the foundation of the Crewdson Prize for Natural Sciences. She is commemorated by the panelling in the dining hall, designed by Mr C. R. Ashbee and carried out by Messrs Rattee and Kett. (See *Girton Review*, Michaelmas Term, 1929.)

*ANDERSON, ELIZABETH GARRETT, 1836–1917, daughter of Newson Garrett, wife of J. G. S. Anderson; the first woman to qualify as a medical practitioner in England. Founder of the first hospital to be staffed by women (now the Elizabeth Garrett Anderson Hospital); for many years Lecturer and Dean of the London School of Medicine for Women. Gave £1000 towards reduction of the building debt at Girton, 1910.

ANDERSON, SIR HUGH KERR, 1865–1928, M.A., M.D., F.R.C.P., F.R.S.; Master of Gonville and Caius College, 1912–28; Member of Royal Commission on Oxford and Cambridge Universities,

1919, and of the Cambridge Statutory Commission, 1923. Member of the Girton College Council, 1913–16, Chairman, 1913–14.

ARNOLD, SIR ARTHUR, 1833–1902; radical politician and writer, a phil-Hellene, and an advocate of the enfranchisement of women. First Editor of the *Echo*, 1868–75; M.P. for Salford, 1880–5; Alderman of the London County Council, 1889–1902, Chairman, 1895 and 1896. Author of *History of the Cotton Famine, Social Politics*, etc. The Sir Arthur Arnold Trust, from which scholarships and exhibitions are awarded, was founded in his memory in 1905, with a gift of £1000 from Lady Arnold.

ASHWORTH HALLETT, LILIAS SOPHIA, of Claverton Lodge, Bath; born about 1841–2; died 1922; daughter of Thomas Ashworth and Sophia, sister to Rt Hon. John Bright; married in 1877 Thomas Palmer George Hallett, Lecturer in Economics at the University of Bristol. Mrs Ashworth Hallett was Hon. Secretary and subsequently Treasurer of the Bristol and West of England Society for Women's Suffrage, 1872–1903; she often spoke for the women's suffrage movement in the days when its supporters were considered hardly respectable. Her social position and personal charm enabled her to serve the movement with much success. She was a member of the Society of Friends. A scholarship at Girton was founded in her memory.

AUSTEN LEIGH, AUGUSTUS, 1840–1905; Provost of King's, 1889–1905; did much to further the reforms by means of which King's College ceased to be a close corporation of Eton collegers, and was thrown open to the world. Member of Girton College, 1880–9, being one of the first Representative Members appointed by the Senate.

AUSTIN, MRS; Mistress of The College, Hitchin, 1870–2; daughter of Mr Crow of Gateshead; wife of Mr T. Austin, architect. Mrs Austin was an early friend of Miss Emily Davies.

AYRTON, HERTHA, 1854–1923, daughter of L. Marks; student at Girton, 1878–81; married (as his second wife) Professor W. E.

Ayrton, F.R.S., in 1885; carried out research in connection with the electric arc, and sand ripples; author of *The Electric Arc*; nominated in 1902 for a Fellowship of the Royal Society, for which however she was ineligible under the conditions of their Charter; awarded the Royal Society's Hughes Medal, 1908. Invented in 1915 an anti-gas fan which was used for the protection of the troops in the war. An active and militant suffragist. She was intimate with Madame Bodichon and with George Eliot, who took the character of Mira in *Daniel Deronda* from her. Elected as Representative Member of Girton College by the Certificated Students, 1886–92. Five pictures by Madame Bodichon belonging to Mrs Ayrton were given to the College after her death by her daughter, Mrs Ayrton Gould, and also her portrait by Helena Darmesteter. (See *Hertha Ayrton*, a memoir by Evelyn Sharp.)

BENTINCK SMITH, MARY, 1864–1921, D.Litt. (T.C.D.); J.P. for the County of Fife; Scholar of Girton, 1890–4; Medieval and Modern Languages Tripos, Class I (with distinction), 1893; Lecturer at Victoria College, Belfast, 1894–7, at Royal Holloway College, 1897–9, at Girton, 1899–1906; Director of Studies, 1902–6; Principal of Avery Hill Training College, 1906–7; Headmistress, St Leonards School, St Andrews, 1907–21. Elected as Representative Member of Girton College by the Certificated Students, 1916–24. Her published work includes an edition of Chaucer's *Prologue* and *Knight's Tale*. The entrance gates of wrought iron at Girton were erected to her memory.

BERNARD, MISS M. F. *See* LATHAM, MRS P. W.

BERRY, ARTHUR, 1863–1929; Scholar of King's College; Senior Wrangler, 1885. It was said that enough marks could have been subtracted from his total in the Tripos to make another wrangler, leaving him still at the head of the list. Fellow of King's, 1886–1929; University Extension Lecturer and later Secretary of the Cambridge organization for University Extension; author of *A Short History of Astronomy* and many mathematical papers. Married in 1902 Miss H. M. Johnson, sister to Mr W. E.

Johnson (Fellow of King's and Sidgwick Lecturer in Moral Sciences). Undertook war service abroad, 1916–18; Vice-Provost of King's, 1924–9. He was most valuable as Vice-Provost during the difficult period of transition from the old order to the new world established by the Royal Commission. He had strong social and political interests. Lecturer at Girton, 1886–1929, Member of the Council, 1900–29, Chairman, 1914–15 and 1919–21. Mr and Mrs Berry (who died four months after her husband) left about £4000 to Girton, and he also left £100 to the Girton library.

BIDDER, MRS, *née* Marion Greenwood, 1862–1932; student at Girton, 1879–83; Natural Sciences Tripos, Part I, Class I, 1882; Part II, Class I, 1883; first winner of the Gamble Prize, 1888. Engaging in biological research, she made a special study of the amoeba, and her work was favourably noticed by Metchnikoff. She held the Bathurst Studentship at Newnham, and was for many years lecturer and demonstrator in physiology and biology at Girton and Newnham; her remarkable ability and organizing power were of great service to both Colleges. She married in 1899 Dr G. P. Bidder of Trinity College; was for many years a Poor Law Guardian; a Liberal and a supporter of women's suffrage. Member of Girton College, 1892–8 and 1918–24, and a Governor of the College, 1924–32. She gave bookcases for the students' rooms in the older buildings.

BLACKBURN, HELEN, 1842–1903, daughter of Bewicke Blackburn (civil engineer and inventor); Secretary to the Central Committee of the National Society for Women's Suffrage, 1874–95; Secretary of the Bristol and West of England Suffrage Society, 1880–95; editor of *The Englishwoman's Review*, 1881–90; author of *Women's Suffrage, a Record of the Movement in the British Isles*, 1902, and of various pamphlets. She bequeathed her library of books on the women's movement to Girton.

*BODICHON, BARBARA LEIGH SMITH, 1827–91, daughter of Benjamin Smith, M.P.; chief originator of the movement for the emancipation of women, in which she worked especially for the suffrage and for education. Studied water-colour painting under

Hunt and Corot; married in 1857 Dr Eugène Bodichon of Algiers. Member of Girton College, 1869–91. (See *Emily Davies and Girton College*, by Barbara Stephen; *Hertha Ayrton*, by Evelyn Sharp; and *Letters to William Allingham*.)

BRYCE, JAMES, 1838–1922, P.C., G.C.V.O., O.M., D.C.L., LL.D., F.R.S., etc.; Assistant Commissioner under the Schools Enquiry Commission, 1864; Regius Professor of Civil Law at Oxford, 1870–93; Liberal M.P., 1880–1907; held Cabinet office in various capacities, 1886–1907; Ambassador at Washington, 1907–13; created Viscount Bryce, 1914. Author of *The Holy Roman Empire*, *The American Commonwealth*, etc. Member of Girton College, 1872–1922.

BUTLER, AGNATA FRANCES, 1867–1931, third daughter of Sir James Ramsay, Bt., of Banff; educated at St Leonards School, St Andrews, where she was a pupil of Mrs Arthur Strong (student at Girton, 1877–82, subsequently Assistant Director of the British School at Rome, and Research Fellow of Girton); Miss Ramsay entered Girton as The Misses Metcalfes' Scholar in 1884. Classical Tripos, Part I, Cl. I, Div. 1, 1887. As a student "she was a very hard worker but delighted in open air and exercise, being good at tennis and excelling in skating.... In debates, though she was President for a period, she did not speak very often, but on occasion she could rise to real eloquence". The "beauty and purity and humility of her mind" made a strong impression on her contemporaries. She married in 1888 Dr H. Montagu Butler, Master of Trinity. After his death in 1918 she continued to live in Cambridge, devoting herself to Christian Science. (See *Girton Review*, Michaelmas Term, 1931 and Lent Term, 1932.)

CAIRNES, JOHN ELLIOTT, 1823–75; Whately Professor of Political Economy at Dublin, 1856–61; subsequently Professor of Political Economy at University College, London. Author of *The Slave Power*, 1866 (a powerful defence of the cause of the Northern American States), *Essays on Political Economy*, and other works. The John Elliott Cairnes Scholarship was founded in his memory by his niece, Miss Robertson.

CARLISLE, ROSALIND, COUNTESS OF, 1845–1921, daughter of the 2nd Lord Stanley of Alderley and of Henrietta Maria Lady Stanley of Alderley; married in 1864 George Howard, afterwards 9th Earl of Carlisle. An able, high-spirited woman, with strong artistic and political interests; with many friends among the Pre-Raphaelites, the French exiles of 1870, and the Liberal party in England; a strong supporter of the temperance movement, of Home Rule for Ireland, and Free Trade. President of the Women's Liberal Federation, and the British Women's Temperance Association. Gave £2000 to Girton in 1904 for the reduction of the building debt, and left £20,000 to the College for scholarships.

CHESSAR, JANE AGNES, 1835–80; a member of the staff of the Home and Colonial College (then at Gray's Inn Road, now at Wood Green), where her power and influence as a teacher did much to bring the College to a high state of efficiency, 1852–66. Lecturer on Elementary Physiology and Hygiene for the National Health Society; member of the London School Board, 1873–5. The J. A. Chessar Classical Scholarship was founded in 1876 in her memory by her pupil, Miss E. T. Minturn, a student at Girton, 1877–80.

COOK, RACHEL SUSAN. *See* SCOTT, MRS C. P.

*COURTNEY, LEONARD HENRY (Lord Courtney of Penwith), 1832–1918; Chairman of Committees in the House of Commons; Member of Girton College, 1876–1918. Bequeathed half his residuary estate (about £19,000) to Girton.

COWELL, EDWARD BYLES, 1826–1903; Professor of Sanskrit at Cambridge, 1867–1903; editor and translator of many Sanskrit texts. He was also versed in Persian, Spanish, Hebrew, Italian, and Welsh literature, as well as in botany and geology. Royal Asiatic Society's Gold Medal; Hon. LL.D. Edinburgh; Hon. D.C.L. Oxford; an original member of the British Academy. He left his library for distribution between Corpus College, the University Library, the Fitzwilliam Museum, and Girton.

CREWDSON, GERTRUDE GWENDOLEN BEVAN, 1872–1913, niece to Mr Alfred Waterhouse (*q.v.*); student at Girton, 1894–7; Librarian and Registrar, 1900–2; Junior Bursar, 1902–5. She purchased the field to the north of the College, on the Girton Road, in 1902, to preserve it from being built over, and bequeathed it to the College. She also left £250 to the Frances Mary Buss loan fund; and she gave the Egyptian antiquities collected by her in Egypt. At her house, Homewood, Woburn Sands, she maintained a holiday home for gentlewomen earning their living. Elected a Representative Member of the College by the Certificated Students, 1898–1901. Hon. Sec. of the Association of Certificated Students from 1908 till 1911, when it was dissolved on the formation of the Roll. (See *Girton Review*, Michaelmas Term, 1913.)

CUNNINGHAM, WILLIAM, D.D., 1849–1919; Scholar of Trinity; bracketed Senior in Moral Sciences Tripos with F. W. Maitland, 1872; Chaplain of Trinity, 1880–91; Vicar of Great St Mary's, 1887–1908; Archdeacon of Ely, 1907–19. A pioneer in the teaching and writing of English economic history, he published the first text-book on the subject, *The Growth of English Industry and Commerce*, 1882; six subsequent editions, and other works on economic and social questions. Tooke Professor of Economics and Statistics, London University, 1891–7; Fellow of Trinity, 1891–1919. Member of Girton College, 1902–14 and 1915–19. Chairman of the Council, 1909–13 and 1915–19. Donor of Publication Fund.

*DAVIES, SARAH EMILY, 1830–1921. In addition to the work at Girton described in the text, Miss Davies took part in the first women's suffrage agitation, 1865–7; was one of the first members of the London School Board, 1870–3; returned to suffrage work in 1904. (See *Emily Davies and Girton College*, by Barbara Stephen.)

DOVE, DAME JANE FRANCES, D.B.E. (cr. 1928), M.A. (T.C.D.); daughter of the Vicar of Cowbitt, Lincs.; student of Girton, 1871–4; Headmistress of St Leonards School, St Andrews,

1882–96; first Headmistress of Wycombe Abbey School, 1896–1910; Member of Girton College, 1902–24. Life Governor of Girton as a Friend of the College under the Charter of 1924.

*FITCH, SIR JOSHUA, 1824–1903, Inspector of Schools; held various important educational appointments; Member of Girton College, 1878–1903.

FRERE, MARY ELIZA ISABELLA, 1845–1911, daughter of Sir Bartle Frere. Living with her father during his Governorship of Bombay, she became interested in Indian folk-lore; and published in 1868 a collection of old stories preserved by oral tradition, *Old Deccan Days*, a charming book, which gave a fresh impetus to the study of folk-lore. She spent the years 1877–80 in South Africa when her father was High Commissioner; later she travelled in Egypt and Palestine, lived at Cambridge, and studied Hebrew. She left her library of Hebrew books to Girton.

FREUND, IDA, 1863–1914, born in Austria, but resident in England from her eighteenth year; student at Girton, 1882–6; Natural Sciences Tripos, Part I, Cl. I, 1885; Part II, Cl. I, 1886; Demonstrator in Chemistry at Newnham College, 1887–93; Staff Lecturer, 1893–1913; Member of Newnham Council, 1896–1903. A remarkable teacher and organizer, she also did valuable research work in Chemistry; her chief published work was *Chemical Composition* (1904). Being awarded the Gamble Prize in 1903, she gave the prize money for the purchase of scientific books and apparatus for the Girton Chemical Laboratory, the Balfour Laboratory, and the Girton Library. (See *Girton Review*, May Term, 1914.)

GAMBLE, JANE CATHERINE, 1808–85; born in Virginia, U.S.A. Her mother died when she was nine months old, and her father having married again, she was sent to England at the age of three, and adopted by her uncle and aunt, Mr and Mrs James Dunlop. She was evidently a clever and cultivated woman, of spirit and strong feelings, affectionate and generous. Being reputed an heiress, she was pursued by a fortune hunter who, with the help of her courier, whom he bribed, tried to abduct her while travelling in Italy in 1851, and shut her up in a palace at Genoa.

She was rescued with the help of a kinsman who came out from England, and the fortune hunter suffered a term of imprisonment. The rest of her life was uneventful; in later years she lived with a companion in London at 67 Portland Place, in a certain amount of old-fashioned state, having a footman standing at the back of her carriage when she drove out. It is known that her painful experience gave her a lasting distrust of men, and this is indicated in her will. Having no very near relations, she left various legacies, including three to god-daughters, and two to her successive companions (the last of whom was with her for ten years). The following condition was attached: "I declare that all legacies given by me to females shall be for their sole and separate use, and free from marital control". Her residuary estate (about £19,000) she left to Girton. The first Married Woman's Property Act was passed in 1882, the year in which she made her will; before that date, a woman on marrying lost her property, which passed into the possession and complete control of her husband. Miss Gamble's attention may well have been drawn to Girton by the success of Miss Scott in the Mathematical Tripos of 1880 (see *ante*, p. 74). Her legacy was the first large sum ever given to the College, and was of great importance, making it possible to purchase seventeen acres of additional land, and to make a large extension of the buildings. The College received as part of her legacy about 400 volumes of English literature, and some Italian marbles, etc. (see p. 165). Sir Francis Chantrey the sculptor, and his wife, appear to have been intimate with her. She died in Florence and is buried at Kensal Green. She was commemorated by the foundation of the Gamble Prize. (See *My Courtship and its Consequences*, by Henry Wikoff, 1855.)

GAMBLE, JOHN, 1859–1929; educated at Trinity College, Dublin, and in Germany; appointed incumbent of St Mary's, Leigh Woods, near Bristol, 1892; residentiary canon of Bristol, 1922; gave much time to the Charity Organization Society and other social work; member of the Governing Body of Bristol University and Chairman of the Redland High School for Girls; a teacher and preacher of much weight and influence; author of *Christ and*

Criticism, The Spiritual Sequence of the Bible, The Sower and other Sermons, etc. (See *ante*, p. 136.)

GARRETT, ELIZABETH. *See* ANDERSON, ELIZABETH GARRETT.

GAVIN, ETHEL; Scholar of Girton, 1885–9; Headmistress successively at Shrewsbury, Notting Hill and Wimbledon High Schools. The Ethel Gavin Prize was founded in her memory by Miss G. Hume in 1918.

GIBSON, EMILY CAROLINE. *See* TOWNSHEND, MRS.

GIBSON, MARGARET DUNLOP, younger twin daughter of John Smith, solicitor, of Paisley. With her twin sister Agnes she studied languages, including modern Greek, Syriac, Hebrew, Arabic, etc. They travelled much and adventurously in the East, gaining access to monastic libraries; on one occasion they were drawn up in a basket to a Coptic monastery on a rock, the abbot next day preaching a sermon in their honour. Margaret married in 1883 James Young Gibson, who had been trained for the Presbyterian ministry, but relinquished his ministry on grounds of health, and thereafter travelled in the East and in Spain, and published translations of the *Cid Ballads*, and other books. He died in 1886. Agnes Smith married in 1887 the Rev. S. S. Lewis of Corpus Christi College, Cambridge, and Mrs Gibson lived with them at Castle Brae, Chesterton, Cambridge. Mr Lewis died in 1891. In 1892 the sisters visited the Convent of St Catherine on Mount Sinai, where they discovered the Syro-Antiochene or Sinaitic palimpsest, the oldest known MS of the Four Gospels. They took about 1000 photographs of it, and deciphered it in co-operation with other scholars. They both received the Hon. LL.D. of St Andrews and also the triennial gold medal of the Royal Asiatic Society, 1915. Residing at Cambridge, they were constant benefactors to the Westminster Presbyterian Training College, and were generous and untiring in their hospitality to a very wide circle. The Gibson Greek Testament Prize was founded by Mrs Gibson in memory of her husband. She died in 1920. (See *How the Codex was Found*, by Mrs Gibson; *The Cid Ballads*, by J. Y. Gibson (with memoir).)

GILES, PETER, Litt.D., Hon. LL.D. Aberdeen; Master of Emmanuel College; Vice-Chancellor of Cambridge University, 1919–21; educated at Aberdeen University, Caius College, Cambridge, Freiburg-im-Breisgau, and Leipzig. University Reader in Comparative Philology; author of *A Short Manual of Comparative Philology* (1905), and of many articles and papers. Member of Girton College, 1918–24; Chairman of the Council, 1921–4; Vice-Chairman and Governor since 1924.

*GOLDSMID, LOUISA LADY, 1819–1909, wife of Sir Francis Goldsmid, a constant supporter of movements for the education and enfranchisement of women. Member of Girton College, 1872–1908; founded the Sir Francis Goldsmid Scholarship, and left about £9000 to the College. (See *Girton Review*, Lent Term, 1909.)

GORST, SIR JOHN, 1835–1916, M.P.; a member with Lord Randolph Churchill, Mr Arthur Balfour (afterwards Earl of Balfour) and Sir H. Drummond Wolff, of the "Fourth Party", 1880–4. M.P. for Cambridge University, 1892–1906. After holding various Government offices he devoted himself to speaking and writing on education and on health. Member of Girton College, 1872–83.

GREENWOOD, MARION. *See* BIDDER, MRS.

GRÜNER, ALICE; student at Newnham College, 1883–6 (sister to Miss Joan Grüner, student at Girton, 1874–7); principal founder of the Women's University Settlement, Southwark; for many years Secretary to the Association of University Women Teachers; gave a benefaction to the Girton Library for the purchase of Russian and Slavonic books.

GURNEY, MARY, 1836–1917, daughter of Joseph Gurney. A founder of the Women's National Educational Union, which in 1872 was merged in the Girls' Public Day School Co.; a supporter of University extension, of Cheltenham College, and of the Princess Helena College. Member of Girton College, 1894–1917. Miss Gurney and her sister, Miss Amelia Gurney, gave £1000 for additions to the Chemical Laboratory at Girton, 1907;

they gave the clocks in the hall and near the chapel, 1910. Miss Mary Gurney founded the Charity Reeves Prize for English, 1910; the sisters bequeathed in all nearly £30,000 to the College. (See *Girton Review*, May Term, 1918.)

*GURNEY, MRS RUSSELL, 1823–96; befriended Miss Davies and Miss Elizabeth Garrett in their attempts to secure medical education for Miss Garrett. Member of Girton College, 1872–96.

HAMILTON GORDON, LADY, 1830–1909, granddaughter of Sir William Herschel the astronomer, married in 1852 Hon. Alexander Gordon (son of Lord Aberdeen, Prime Minister); Woman of the Bedchamber to Queen Victoria, 1855–1901; interested in Girton since 1874, when her sister Constance Herschel (now Lady Lubbock) entered the College as a student. Lady Hamilton Gordon gave to Girton the Gold Medal presented to her great aunt, Caroline Herschel, by the Royal Astronomical Society.

HANCOCK, OTTILIE, daughter of Karl Blind, German politician and writer, who after taking part in the revolutionary movements of 1848–9 lived as an exile in England till his death in 1907. His young family (including his step-daughter, Mathilde Blind the poetess) became English in education and sympathies. Ottilie in her youth knew Mazzini, Karl Marx, Louis Blanc, and other political exiles, friends of her father. She married Charles Hancock, and was an active supporter of Home Rule, Women's Suffrage, and the League of Nations; organized working parties for the Serbian Red Cross during the war, 1914–18; died in 1929. She had previously endowed two Fellowships at Girton, one named after herself, and one after her friend Mrs Ayrton (*q.v.*).

HASTINGS, GEORGE; Secretary to the Law Amendment Society (founded 1844), through which the first attempt was made to reform the laws relating to married women's property; Secretary to the National Association for the Promotion of Social Science (founded 1857), which did much to help the women's movement; member of the Committee formed in 1862 to secure the admission of women to University examinations; member of the Committee for the foundation of a College for women (afterwards Girton College), 1867–70.

HERSCHEL, CAROLINE LUCRETIA, 1750–1848; astronomer, sister of Sir William Herschel, born at Hanover; received in youth only the first elements of education and was employed in household duties till 1772, when she joined her brother who had established himself as organist and music teacher at Bath. She helped him with his musical work and in astronomical research, and when he became astronomer to George III she became his assistant, receiving a salary of £50 a year from the King (1787). She detected three nebulae (1783), and eight comets (1786–97); and presented to the Royal Society an Index to Flamsteed's Observations, and a catalogue of 561 stars accidentally omitted from the *British Catalogue* (1797). The Astronomical Society presented her with their gold medal (now at Girton) in 1828, and elected her an honorary member (1835).

HEYWOOD, JAMES, 1810–97, son of a Unitarian banker in Manchester; educated at Bristol, Edinburgh, and Geneva. Entered his father's bank, 1828, but inheriting a fortune retired and entered Trinity College, Cambridge. Qualified for B.A. degree but was debarred from taking it by the religious test. Studied science, especially geology; F.R.S., 1837; called to the Bar; Liberal M.P. for North Lancs., 1847–57. An active worker for removal of religious tests; he took his degree when this object was secured. Translated and edited Heer's *Primaeval World of Switzerland*, and von Bohlen's *Introduction to the Book of Genesis*, published Haber and Newman's *English Universities*. President of Royal Statistical Society, 1876; Chairman of the Royal Historical Society's Council, 1878. Fellow and Member of the Governing Body of London University; supported the admission of women to that University and to the suffrage. Founder and first President of the Sunday Society (for freedom from restriction). Founded and maintained the Heywood Public Library in Kensington, 1874, till in 1887 it was handed over to the Public Library Commissioners. Member of Girton College, 1872–97. Gave a water-colour picture of Cambridge market-place by Louise Rayner to the College in 1883.

JACKSON, GERTRUDE ELIZABETH MATHER, daughter of Sir Henry Jackson; educated at Miss Metcalfe's school; student at Girton, 1876–80; elected Representative Member of the College by Certificated Students, 1884–1905; co-opted Member, 1905–18; Junior Bursar, 1891–7. In 1892 she initiated the Old Students' Studentship Fund for research. She was a founder of the University Women's Club, and of the Wellbrook Laundry. In later years she lived in Monmouthshire and interested herself in country work, particularly in placing women on the land during the war, and in Women's Institutes. She died in 1919. (See *Girton Review*, May Term, 1920.)

JACKSON, HENRY, 1839–1921, O.M., Litt.D., Fellow of Trinity College, Cambridge, 1864–1921; Regius Professor of Greek, 1906–21; Vice-Master of Trinity College, 1914–19; a Member of Girton College, 1875–1921. Supported the admission of women to the University on the same terms as men. (See *Henry Jackson, O.M.*, by Dr R. St John Parry.)

JONES, EMILY ELIZABETH CONSTANCE; educated at home, and for one year (1866–7) at Miss Robinson's school, Alston Court, near Cheltenham. Student at Girton, 1875–80; Moral Sciences Tripos, Class I, 1880; Resident Lecturer in Moral Sciences, 1884–1916; Librarian, 1890–3; Vice-Mistress, 1896–1903; Mistress and Director of Studies in Moral Sciences, 1903–16. She completed Miss Hamilton's translation of Lotze's *Microcosmus*, and was the author of *Elements of Logic*, and *New Law of Thought*, and various articles on philosophical subjects. After retiring from Girton she did much to encourage University extension in Somerset. She died in 1922. (See *Girton Review*, May Term, 1922; and *What I Remember*, by E. E. C. Jones.)

KENSINGTON, FRANCES, 1851–1931, daughter of Arthur Kensington (Fellow and Tutor of Trinity College, Oxford); educated at home, where she learned Latin and Greek as well as modern languages, and became well read in English literature. About 1864 she attended the French classes of Anton Roche, and German classes of Dr Kinkel, an exile of 1848, later she followed the courses of the Home Study Society, through which she was taught by F. H. W. Myers, A. W. Verrall, and other excellent teachers. After some years of social work in London, and as Secretary to Bedford College, she became Secretary to Girton College, 1882–97; Bursar, 1894–7; Member of Girton College, 1893–1924; and a Life Governor as a Friend of the College under the Charter of 1924. She was a member of the Wycombe Abbey School Council from its foundation, a Reid Trustee (Bedford College), and Secretary to the Paddington Girl Guides. An excellent walker, an active enterprising and courageous traveller, she was youthful in spirit to the end of her long life. (See *Girton Review*, Easter Term, 1931.)

KNOWLES, PROFESSOR LILIAN, daughter of Philip Tomn; student at Girton, 1890–4; Class I in the Historical Tripos, 1893, and in the Law Tripos, 1894. Pupil of Archdeacon Cunningham, with whom she co-operated in his book, *The Growth of English Industry and Commerce*. Married Charles Knowles, 1904; appointed Lecturer at the London School of Economics, 1904; Reader of Economic History in the University of London, 1907; Professor, 1919; Dean of the Faculty of Economics, 1920 (the first woman to be Dean of a Faculty); member of the Council of the Royal Economic Society; member of the Departmental Committee on the Rise of the Cost of Living to the Working Classes, 1918; member of Royal Commission on Income Tax, 1919–20; author of *The Industrial and Commercial Revolutions in Great Britain* (1919), *The Economic Development of the Overseas Empire* (1921). (See *Girton Review*, May Term, 1926.)

LATHAM, MRS P. W., daughter of Dr Bernard of Bristol; Mistress of Girton, 1875–85; married Dr P. W. Latham of Cambridge, 1885; died 1925. "This lady, who is a niece of Lord Lawrence's [the Viceroy of India], seems to unite all the qualities of character and attainment which will fit her for a position of influence over younger women at a moment when many difficulties still beset an institution so novel in its character as Girton College" (*Journal of the Women's Educational Union*, July 15th, 1875). Member of the College, 1885–1924; Life Governor as a Friend of the College under the Charter of 1924. (See *ante*, Chapter v; and *Girton Review*, May Term, 1926.)

LIVEING, GEORGE DOWNING, F.R.S., 1827–1924; father of scientific (especially chemical) studies at Cambridge; entered St John's College, 1847; 11th Wrangler, 1850; first in order of merit in recently instituted Natural Sciences Tripos, 1851; studied in Berlin; Fellow of St John's College, 1853. A College lectureship was founded for him, and a laboratory built, and he was the first man to teach science experimentally in Cambridge. Appointed Professor at the Staff College and at Sandhurst, 1860; married Catherine Ingram and consequently vacated his Fellowship. Professor of Chemistry at Cambridge, 1861–1908. In 1863 the University began to build laboratories, in the design of which he took a large part; when completed in 1888 they were some of the finest in the country. Took a prominent part in the movement for University reform in the 'eighties. President of St John's College, 1911–24. Member of Girton College, 1880–94 (one of the first representative members appointed by the Senate), and a Life Governor as a Friend of the College under the Charter of 1924. A constant supporter of the admission of women to the University.

LLOYD, ANNA, 1837–1925, ninth child of Samuel Lloyd of Wood Green, Wednesbury, a member of the Society of Friends. After her parents' death, she had no settled home, and in 1868, during a visit to Miss Davies's friend, Miss Anna Richardson, she was persuaded to enter The College, Hitchin. "I cannot think what made Miss Davies so set upon me with her resolute determination I should enter", she wrote to a friend. "She has her way. My sisters and friends look on astonished—it is such a new sensation. They say I must go my own way, they cannot judge for me; but I see they think it would be much better if I was going to be married." After four terms at the College, she left it reluctantly, partly owing to ill health, partly in deference to the wishes of her sisters, who believed that family claims should be the first consideration of any unmarried woman. She made her home with her brother Henry near Wednesbury till his marriage in 1895; was Guardian of the Poor (the only woman member) at West Bromwich, 1888–92; later settled at Edgbaston, visiting Italy frequently. A warm friendship with Ruskin, who taught her painting, led to friendship with Francesca Alexander, author of *Wayside Songs of Tuscany*. Anna Lloyd had strong religious, literary, and artistic interests, and was a skilled painter and embroiderer. "She was very responsive; it was always worth while to make a suggestion, for her festive spirit would catch hold of it at once." (See *Anna Lloyd, a Memoir*, by Edyth M. Lloyd.)

LUMSDEN, DAME LOUISA INNES, D.B.E. (cr. 1925), Hon. LL.D. St Andrews; educated at private schools in London and Brussels; student at The College, Hitchin, 1869–72; Classical Tripos, 1892; Classical Tutor at Girton, 1873–4; at Cheltenham Ladies' College, 1876–7; first Headmistress of St Leonards School, St Andrews, 1877–82; Member and Chairman of two School Boards in Aberdeenshire, 1888–90; first Warden of University Hall for Women Students, St Andrews, 1895–1900. Life Governor of Girton as a Friend of the College under the Charter of 1924.

LUMSDEN, MARY; student at Girton, 1893–6; worked for many years in connection with Miss Octavia Hill at Walworth. In 1914 she worked with the Society of Friends in re-settling farmers and peasants in the Marne Valley after the withdrawal of the Germans. She also worked for the Ministry of Munitions housing schemes; and organized a market garden carried on by women in Surrey. Later she spent some years in China, occupying herself with relief and philanthropic works. Governor of Girton College and Member of the Council, 1916–23. She died in 1931, and bequeathed £1000 to the College.

McARTHUR, ELLEN ANNETTE, 1862–1927; daughter of the Rector of Burlingham, Norfolk; educated in Germany and at

St Leonards School under Dame Louisa Lumsden; Scholar of Girton, 1882–5; Historical Tripos, Cl. I; lecturer at Girton, 1886–1907; first woman appointed as lecturer to the Cambridge Local Lectures Syndicate, and as examiner for Oxford and Cambridge Schools Examination Board. Lectured on Economic History to men and women students at Cambridge, 1902–12; Litt.D. Dublin, 1905; F.R.Hist.S. 1906; Supervisor of History Department, Westfield College, 1907–10; member of the Faculty of Arts and of the Historical Board, University of London. Hon. Secretary and Chairman of the Cambridge Training College for Teachers for some years after 1896; an Hon. Member of Newnham College. Representative Member of Girton College elected by Certificated Students, 1907–10; collaborated with Archdeacon Cunningham in *The Growth of English Industry and Commerce* and other books; author of many historical papers. A keen supporter of women's suffrage. (See *Girton Review*, Michaelmas Term, 1927.)

MANNING, E. ADELAIDE, daughter of Mr Serjeant Manning by his first wife; a student at The College, Hitchin, Michaelmas Term, 1869; Member of Girton College, 1873–1905; for many years Hon. Secretary to the National Indian Association. She bequeathed £2000 to Girton, also the Kaisar-i-Hind Medal given to her for services in connection with India, some pieces of Indian silver presented to her, and an early portrait of Mrs Manning. She gave three water-colour drawings by Richard Doyle (designer of the cover of *Punch*) to Girton. Her portrait (painted from a photograph) was presented by Miss Davies.

*MANNING, CHARLOTTE, daughter of Isaac Solly, wife of Mr Serjeant Manning. Mistress of The College, Hitchin, for the Michaelmas Term, 1869. Commemorated by the clock in the Emily Davies Court.

*METCALFE, FANNY; Headmistress of Highfield School, Hendon, founded 1863. Member of Girton College, 1872–96; died 1897.

MEYER, MARGARET THEODORA; born in Ireland, spent much of her childhood in Italy; educated at North London Collegiate

School under Miss Buss; student at Girton, 1879–82; Mathematical Tripos, 1882; taught at Notting Hill High School; Resident Lecturer at Girton, 1888–1918; Director of Studies, 1903–18; Member of the College, 1908–11. During the war she worked at calculations connected with aeroplanes, and visited at the First Eastern Hospital. One of the first women Fellows of the Royal Astronomical Society; an early member of the Ladies' Alpine Club (1909); served on its Committee, 1912–22, and as President, 1916–19. After retiring from Girton she taught privately and at University College, London, and interested herself in L.C.C. Care Committee work, and in Indian students. Died in 1924. Her interest in the College chapel is commemorated by the panelling in the chancel, carved partly by herself and partly by old students under her direction; and carried round the rest of the chapel as a memorial after her death. She left £2000 to the College for the encouragement of mathematics, £1000 for general purposes, and a collection of mathematical books. (See *Girton Review*, May Term, 1924.)

MINET, JULIA, 1842–1924, eldest daughter of James L. Minet of 18 Sussex Square, London. During her long life she was specially devoted to all social questions, Housing, M.A.B.Y.S., Charity Organization, and not least to education as a manager of a London School. She was a direct descendant of Isaac Minet, a Huguenot refugee of 1686. She bequeathed £2000 to be applied for the benefit of resident lecturers and administrative officers of the College.

MONTEFIORE, THÉRÈSE ALICE, daughter of L. Schorstein; student at Girton, 1882–5; married Mr Claude G. Montefiore; died 1889. Mr Montefiore has identified himself with philanthropic and educational work, especially in connection with the Anglo-Jewish Association, the Froebel Educational Institute, and University College, Southampton. He was Hibbert Lecturer in 1892, and has published many works on Biblical history and criticism. He married, secondly, Miss Florence Ward; Librarian at Girton, 1884–8; Junior Bursar, 1889–91; Vice-Mistress,

1885–95. Mr Montefiore founded the Thérèse Montefiore Memorial Prize in 1891.

MÜLLER, HENRIETTA; student at Girton, 1874–7; member of the London School Board, 1879–85; an active feminist; gave some furniture to the College, and some water-colour drawings by John Varley. (See *Girton Review*, Lent Term, 1906.)

NEWALL, DAME BERTHA SURTEES, 1877–1932, D.B.E., Litt.D. (T.C.D.), F.R.Hist.S., Fellow of the Royal Society of Northern Antiquaries, Fellow of the Royal Anthropological Institute; daughter of J. S. Phillpotts, Headmaster of Bedford School. Mistress of Girton, 1922–5; married in 1931 H. F. Newall, F.R.S. (Professor of Astrophysics, 1909–28, and Fellow of Trinity College, Cambridge). Member of the Boards of the Faculties of Modern and Medieval Languages, English, and Archaeology and Anthropology; Examiner for the Archaeological and Anthropological Tripos (Section B), 1928, 1929, 1931. (See *ante*, Chapter VII; and *Girton Review*, Easter Term, 1932.)

PFEIFFER, EMILY JANE; poetess and feminist, 1827–90; daughter of R. Davis (an officer in the army, owner of property in Oxfordshire); married in 1853 J. E. Pfeiffer, a German merchant resident in London. Author of *Valisneria*, *Gerard's Monument*, *Sonnets and Songs*, etc. In 1888 she published *Woman and Work*, a collection of articles from various periodicals. She left money to trustees for the higher education of women, £5000 of which was allotted to Girton.

PHILLPOTTS, DAME BERTHA SURTEES. *See* NEWALL, DAME BERTHA SURTEES.

*PONSONBY, MARY ELIZABETH, wife of Sir Henry Ponsonby; Private Secretary to Queen Victoria. Member of Girton College from 1872 till her death in 1916. The Mary Elizabeth Ponsonby Prize was founded in her memory by her family.

ROBERTS, SIR OWEN, 1835–1915, Fellow of Jesus College, Oxford; Clerk to the Worshipful Company of Clothworkers, 1866–1907; Master, 1909; a pioneer of technical education at the Yorkshire College, Leeds, and at University College, Bristol. At his suggestion Miss Davies applied to the Clothworkers' Company for financial help for Girton, and since 1874 the Company has given an annual Scholarship, and many other benefactions, including £500 towards the reduction of the building debt, 1913. (See *Girton Review*, Lent Term, 1915.)

*ROBY, HENRY JOHN, 1830–1915; Secretary of the Schools Enquiry Commission, 1864; M.P. for Eccles division of Lancashire, 1890–5; Member of Girton College, 1872–1905. (See *Girton Review*, Lent Term, 1915.)

SARGANT, ETHEL, 1863–1918; educated at the North London Collegiate School; student at Girton, 1881–5; Natural Sciences Tripos, Parts I and II. Worked for a year under Dr D. H. Scott at Kew, 1892; afterwards lived at Reigate with her family, working at botanical research in her private laboratory. Author of many botanical papers; one of the first women admitted as a Fellow of the Linnean Society, and the first to serve on its Council. President of a Section of the British Association, 1913; elected Hon. Life Fellow of Girton, 1913; elected Representative Member of Girton College by Certificated Students, 1914–18. President of the Federation of University Women, 1918. Organized a Register of University Women qualified to do work of national importance during the war, which was afterwards taken over by the Ministry of Labour. Bequeathed her botanical library and bookcases to the College. (See *Girton Review*, Lent Term, 1918; Michaelmas Term, 1927.)

SCOTT, CHARLOTTE ANGAS, 1858–1931; D.Sc. Lond.; daughter of Rev. Caleb Scott (Principal of the Lancashire Independent College, Whalley Range, and later the successor of Dr Joseph Parker at the City Temple); student at Girton, 1876–80; equal to eighth wrangler, 1880 (the first woman wrangler); Resident Lecturer at Girton, 1880–4; Associate Professor (1885–8) and Professor (1885–1917) of Mathematics at Brynmawr College, U.S.A.; author of mathematical papers in various journals. Presented Silver Challenge Cup for the Girton and Newnham Lawn Tennis Doubles, 1883.

Scott, Mrs C. P., 1848–1905; daughter of Professor Cook of St Andrews; student at The College, Hitchin, 1869–72; Classical Tripos, 1872; married Mr C. P. Scott of the *Manchester Guardian*, 1873. Member of Girton College, elected by Certificated Students, 1877–80. Member of Committee of Manchester High School for Girls from its foundation; organized higher education for women by means of classes at Manchester, 1877, which led to the admission of women to Owens College, 1883; member of Manchester School Board, 1890–6. (See *Girton Review*, Michaelmas Term, 1905.)

Seeley, Sir John Robert, 1834–95; Professor of Modern History at Cambridge, 1869–95; a University Reformer; author of *Ecce Homo, The Expansion of England, The Life and Times of Stein*, etc.

de Selincourt, Agnes, 1872–1917; student at Girton, 1891–4; Medieval and Modern Languages Tripos, Cl. I; taught at Sheffield High School; studied Oriental Languages at Somerville College; went to Bombay in 1896 to start a missionary settlement for University women; subsequently Principal of the Lady Muir Memorial College, Allahabad. Returned to England and worked for the Student Christian Movement; Principal of Westfield College, 1913–17. (See *Girton Review*, Michaelmas Term, 1917.)

Shaen, William, 1820–87; son of Samuel Shaen of Hatfield Peverel; of Nonconformist stock; educated at University College, London, and Edinburgh. Gold Medal in Philosophy, London, 1842; Fellow of University College; Solicitor to the Girls' Public Day School Company, and to Girton College from its foundation. His experience with the business of Bedford College and other institutions, and his wide views as regards the future development of women's work, made his services particularly valuable, especially in the drafting of Trust Deeds. A leader in the movement begun in 1848 for obtaining a building for London University, and for giving graduates a voice in its government. Clerk to the newly created London Convocation, 1858–68, and subsequently a member of the Annual Committee of the Senate. A founder of Bedford

College for Women and of the London School of Medicine for Women. A constant supporter of the admission of women to the suffrage, and of the removal of their legal disabilities. A devoted friend to Mazzini, and a supporter of many religious, educational and philanthropic undertakings. (See *William Shaen*, a brief sketch, edited by his daughter, M. J. Shaen.)

SHEFFIELD, LORD (4th Baron), 1839–1925, Edward Lyulph Stanley, son of Lord Stanley of Alderley and Henrietta Maria Lady Stanley of Alderley; Fellow of Balliol College, Oxford, 1862; Assistant Commissioner, Friendly Societies' Commission, 1872; M.P. for Oldham, 1880–5; Member of Royal Commission on Housing, 1884; on Elementary Education, 1887; Member of London School Board, 1876–85 and 1888–96. Member of Girton College, 1895–1924; Life Governor as a Friend of the College under the Charter of 1924. Presented the copy of Lady Stanley's portrait by Richmond.

*SHIRREFF, EMILY, 1814–97; a founder of the National Union for improving the education of women of all classes, out of which grew the Girls' Public Day School Company, 1872; Mistress of The College, Hitchin, Lent and Easter Terms, 1870; Member of the College Committee, 1870–2; Member of Girton College, 1872–97.

SIDGWICK, HENRY, 1838–1900; one of the founders of Newnham College; Fellow of Trinity, 1859–69; Knightbridge Professor of Moral Philosophy, 1883–1900. Mrs Henry Sidgwick was Principal of Newnham College, 1892–1910.

*SOMERVILLE, MARY, 1780–1872 (wife of Dr William Somerville); author of *The Connection of the Physical Sciences*, a passage in which suggested to Professor Adams the calculations from which he deduced the orbit of Neptune. Her mathematical library was presented to Girton by her daughters, her bust by Frances Power Cobbe, and her portrait (by S. Laurence) by Lady Stanley of Alderley.

STANLEY, LADY AUGUSTA, daughter of Thomas Bruce, 7th Earl of Elgin (who acquired the "Elgin marbles" for the nation); entered the household of the Duchess of Kent, mother of Queen Victoria; afterwards Resident Bedchamber Woman to the Queen, with whom she was on terms of affectionate friendship. Married in 1863 Dr A. P. Stanley, Dean of Westminster; died 1876. Member of the first Executive Committee of the College for Women, and an original member of Girton College.

*STANLEY OF ALDERLEY, HENRIETTA MARIA, LADY, 1807–95, daughter of Lord Dillon, wife of the second Lord Stanley of Alderley, who held government office under Lord Melbourne and Lord Palmerston; Member of Girton College, 1872–95. She gave the first chemical laboratory at Girton, and the Stanley Library, the bow window in the old dining hall, the lodge by the front gate, and many lesser gifts.

STEVENSON, MAY MARGARET, 1875–1922, O.B.E.; educated at Notting Hill High School and Girton; worked at the Women's University Settlement, Southwark, 1902–17; representative of Girton students on the Settlement Committee, 1909–19; joined the W.A.A.C. on its formation, 1917; died in 1922 of tubercular disease contracted on war service. Bequeathed £500 to Girton.

SWANWICK, ANNA, 1813–99, daughter of John Swanwick of Liverpool; educated privately and at a school at Liverpool. At eighteen she became a pupil of Dr James Martineau (then Unitarian minister at Liverpool, and lecturer on Mental and Moral Philosophy); studied in Berlin; published translations, *Selections from the Dramas of Goethe and Schiller*, 1843; Goethe's *Faust*, 1851; the Trilogy of Aeschylus, 1865, etc.; organized classes and social evenings for poor girls; joined in the movement for Colleges for working men and women; took part in the government of Queen's and Bedford Colleges for women; supported the women's suffrage movement. Hon. LL.D. Aberdeen, 1899.

*TAYLOR, SEDLEY, 1834–1920; Fellow of Trinity College, Cambridge, 1861; President of C.U.M.S.; Member of the Cambridge

Committee in connection with The College, Hitchin; Member of Girton College, 1872–1920. He gave an Organ Scholarship in 1910, and 170 bound volumes of miniature orchestral scores by great masters, 1911.

TODD, MAUDE MARGARET; student at Girton, 1879–82; married Lord Sumner, 1892; founded the Todd Memorial Scholarship in memory of her parents, Dr and Mrs Todd, of Tudor Hall School, Sydenham.

TOMN, LILIAN CHARLOTTE ANN. *See* KNOWLES, PROFESSOR LILIAN.

TOWNSHEND, MRS, *née* Gibson; educated at Miss Pipe's School at Clapham, but had to leave at fifteen owing to financial difficulties. The first applicant for admission to the College for Women (afterwards Girton), of which she heard from a Russian lady in Heidelberg, through whom she got into touch with Lady Augusta Stanley. Student at The College, Hitchin, 1869–72; married C. Townshend (brother to Isabella Townshend, *q.v.*), 1873.

TOWNSHEND, ISABELLA FRANCES; student at The College, Hitchin, 1869–72. With strong artistic perceptions and interests, Miss Townshend was a woman of marked personality and exercised a notable influence among her fellow-students, to some of whom (especially Anna Lloyd) she introduced ideas and interests quite new to them. "Her clear thoughts flow like a crystal stream, if one strikes into one of her subjects", Miss Lloyd wrote of her in 1877. She settled in Rome as a student of painting; and died of typhoid fever in 1882.

TUBBS, FANNY CECILIA, 1831–1921, eldest daughter of Charles William Minet of Baldwyns, Dartford; married in 1861 Colonel R. T. N. Tubbs. Keenly interested in education, she became the first woman member of the School Board of Hastings, where she lived, 1861–1921. As her maiden name shows, she was of Huguenot descent. She was a subscriber to Girton in early days, and for many years a "local referee" for the College.

TURLE, SOPHIA ADELAIDE, 1841–1923, daughter of James Turle (organist of Westminster Abbey); a keen supporter of women's rights, and a subscriber to Girton from very early days. Founded a Musical Scholarship at Girton, 1914, gave £500 to the College, 1923, and made it her residuary legatee. (See *Girton Review*, May Term, 1924.)

WATERHOUSE, ALFRED, 1830–1905; architect of Girton; began practice in Manchester, where he won the competition for the Assize Courts 1859, and designed the Town Hall, Owens College, etc. He became one of the most eminent architects of his time; F.R.I.B.A. 1861; President, 1888–91; Gold Medallist, 1878; R.A. 1885. The Natural History Museum is one of the many buildings in London designed by him. His work at Cambridge includes the Union, and additions to Caius, Trinity Hall, Jesus, and Pembroke. He made additions to Balliol College, Oxford, and designed many great houses such as Eaton Hall and Iwerne Minster. He designed the earliest buildings at Girton; his son, Mr Paul Waterhouse, who became his partner in 1891, collaborated in later additions.

*WELSH, ELIZABETH, 1843–1921; born in Co. Down, a descendant of John Knox; educated at home and at private schools and classes, and by the vicar of her parish; Scholar at The College, Hitchin, and at Girton, 1871–3; Classical Lecturer at Girton, 1876–84; Vice-Mistress, 1880–5; Mistress, 1885–1903; Garden Steward, 1883–1903; Member of the College, 1885–1916. Her grave is in Girton churchyard. (See *ante*, Chapters v and ix.)

WOODHEAD, SARAH, daughter of a grocer in Manchester, and a member of the Society of Friends; a girl of charming looks and refined character, she was well educated at a Quaker school, on leaving which she engaged in teaching, but became a student at The College, Hitchin, 1869–72; Mathematical Tripos, 1872. Returned to teaching and had a school of her own at Bolton; married in 1875 Christopher Corbett (member of a firm of Architects and Surveyors); died 1912.

WRIGHT, ROBERT SAMUEL; Judge of the Queen's Bench Division of the High Court, 1891–1904. Gave substantial help to Girton in scholarships, 1876 and 1877; Member of the College, 1878–1900.

YARROW, SIR ALFRED, 1842–1931; F.R.S.; LL.D. Glasgow; educated at University College School, London; founder of Yarrow and Co., Ltd.; shipbuilder and engineer at Poplar, 1866; on the Clyde, 1906. He was deeply interested in the encouragement of scientific research, for which he gave £100,000 to the Royal Society. He gave £12,000 to Girton for the reduction of the building debt, 1913; and £10,000 for scientific research, 1919. He and Lady Yarrow were made Life Governors as Friends of the College under the Charter of 1924. (See *Alfred Yarrow, his life and work*, by E. C. Barnes [Lady Yarrow].)

INDEX